PROFESSOR THOMAS BILLINGSLEY "T.B." LOGGINS TENNESSEE EDUCATOR AND HIS FAMILY

Written & Compiled by
Gwendolyn "Gwen" McCaffrey McReynolds

Memphis, Tennessee, 2016

Professor Thomas Billingsley "T.B." Loggins
Tennessee Educator
And His Family

Researched and Compiled by Gwendolyn "Gwen" McCaffrey McReynolds who is the great granddaughter of his brother, Henry Mitchell Loggins. "Completed" September 16, 2016.

The following book brings a wide variety of cited sources together for the purpose of creating a tribute to T. B. Loggins. Please be mindful of giving credit to both Gwendolyn McCaffrey McReynolds and the original source if you use parts of this publication.

First Edition: October 2016

ISBN 10: 1945929022
ISBN 13: 978-1945929021

"Uncle T. B.'s school" was what my Grandfather Loggins would say when I asked him where he went to school. As a child and young adult I loved to look at the picture of my very tall grandfather standing on the porch of that school. Although the picture is in black and white, I knew from many discussions with my grandmother that Granddaddy Reuben Wilson Loggins had thick red hair. My focus was so much on him that I never asked who the others were standing with him or even what year the picture was taken. I knew from the tone of Granddaddy's voice that Uncle T. B. was a much loved person in the family but it has been since my retirement from teaching that I have begun to delve into Uncle T. B.'s life. Since Uncle T. B. and Aunt Addie had but one child, Beth, who had no children of her own, I must not let them be lost to time. *(Beth Campbell Loggins, 3rd from left, stands in front of her first cousin, Reuben Wilson Loggins, 4th from the left) on the front porch of Dickson Normal College)*

THOMAS BILLINGSLEY LOGGINS' YOUNG YEARS

Thomas Billingsley Loggins was the third son born to Reuben Burch and Mary Elizabeth Trotter Loggins. He was born in Lodi, Choctaw County, Mississippi October 1, 1862. His father, his uncle (William Thomas Loggins), and his Grandfather (Henry Loggins) were all prosperous cotton farmers with numerous slaves. The 1860 Slave census for Choctaw County, Mississippi lists thirteen female slaves of the following ages 35, 30, 27, 25, 19, 14, 13, 11, 10, 10, 3, 4, 4 and seven male slaves of the following ages 32, 20, 15, 2, 1, 8/12, 8/12 for R. B. Loggins.

On March 22, 1862 less than six months before T. B.'s birth, Reuben Burch joined Company C of the 30th Mississippi Infantry as a sergeant. In addition, T.B.'s Uncle W. T. was the lieutenant and his Aunt Susannah Loggins Billingsley's husband, Thomas Billingsley, for whom T. B. was named, served as the captain of the Choctaw Planters. T. B.'s grandfather, Henry, also served as a recruiter for the unit. [Source: Muster Rolls for 30th Mississippi Infantry on Fold3.com.]

T. B. probably saw little of his father during the years of the War Between the States. Muster Rolls show that the 30th Mississippi joined the war effort shortly after the Battle of Shiloh at the Battle of Chickasaw Bayou, Mississippi on 27 December 1862. (The 1916 application of T. B.'s daughter Beth Loggins Rogers for United Daughters of the Confederacy lists Shiloh as one of the battles in which her grandfather fought, but as of this writing I have found no other written document supporting that claim.) Company C had devastating loses at the Battle of Murfreesboro including Captain Thomas Billingsley who died as a prisoner of war 13 January 1863. The 30th Mississippi served under Walthall throughout most of the war and fought in the major campaigns of the Western Theater. There was one official record that shows Reuben Burch receiving a furlough to go home in January 1865. As a result of this visit home, T.B.'s younger brother, Reuben Burch Loggins, Jr. was born 23 September 1865. Reuben Burch served until Johnston's surrender but he was listed with the 24th Mississippi since there were very few remaining members of the 30th Mississippi. The remaining men from the 30th Mississippi had been reorganized into the 24th Mississippi on April 9, 1865. [The 1904 Walthall Brigade Reunion book that is in the Vivian Loggins McLemore Papers at the Mississippi State Archives states that there were only six of the original company that surrendered. T.B.'s Uncle. Lt. W. T., had been sent home ill before the surrender.] According to the Loggins' family history in the WPA History of Montgomery County, Mississippi (Mississippi State Archives), T.B.'s grandfather, Henry, oversaw the running of his sons' plantations while they were off serving in the war. [Note: Lodi, Mississippi became part of the newly formed Montgomery County, Mississippi in 1871.)

Shortly after the war, T. B. suffered the losses of his daddy's sister, Susannah Loggins Billingsley, on 3 September 1866, his Uncle W. T. on 29 July 1869, his nine year old cousin, Emma, who was the daughter of W. T. on 30 July 1870,

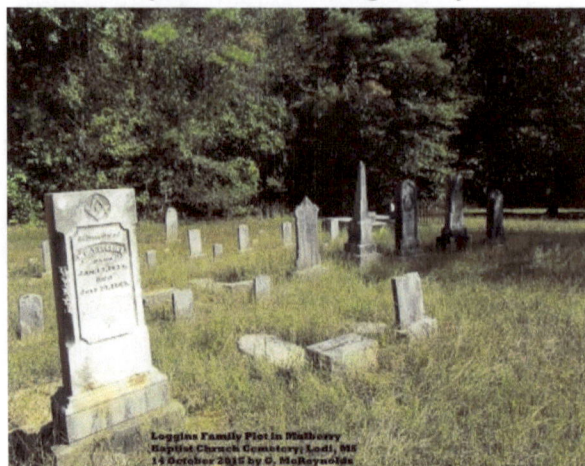

Loggins Family Plot in Mulberry Baptist Church Cemetery; Lodi, MS 14 October 2015 by C. McReynolds

his paternal great grandmother, Susannah Emmerson Loggins Braswell, on 20 July 1871 and his paternal grandmother, Elizabeth S. Darden Loggins, on 19 January 1871. W.T.'s wife, Mary Victoria Cunningham Loggins Hart died 3 August 1871. There had been many trips to the Mulberry Baptist Church Cemetery in Lodi during those five years. [*picture: front left: W. T. Loggins, Emma Loggins, Mary Victoria Cunningham Loggins Hart. 2nd row standing stone: Susannah Emmerson Loggins Braswell, Henry Loggins, Elizabeth S. Darden Loggins, Susannah Loggins Billingsley.*] The source of spelling for Great Grandmother Susannah's maiden name is the Loggins section of the WPA Montgomery County, Mississippi History.

There are no early records that show where T. B. began school but Lodi had a school. One of the founders of the Lodi Academy was T. B.'s grandfather, Henry. The WPA Montgomery County History lists R. B. and W. T. associated with the school, too, as well as Trotter cousins. The description of the school in the June 1937 WPA history is as follows:

> *"The frame building today stands on its original foundations of limestone rock just as it was constructed many years ago. Originally it had two stories, each 12 feet high, 40X 60 feet. It was never painted, and the weather boarding is still in a good state of preservation. The upper story being used by the Masonic Fraternity as a lodge hall; the lower as a schoolroom. A four foot partition across the building separated the girls from the boys."*

Henry sold the Lodi Academy building for the continuing purpose of education to W. H. Parker, Superintendant of Public Education for the newly formed Montgomery County in December 1871. "*six acres of land...in Township 20, R 7 east....to be called the Montgomery County Lodi Academy.*" The deed states that Henry had donated the second floor to the Masons so they had right to meet in the school building. Henry was a Mason. He also served as a Supervisor for the newly formed Montgomery county, Mississippi but the exact date that Henry began is unknown at this writing. By November 1873 he signed a deed noting that he was a Supervisor for Montgomery County. (Records in Winona, Montgomery County, Tennessee Deed Book A)

Exactly when R. B. and Mary Elizabeth Trotter Loggins moved their family of six boys (William Nicholas, born 5 August 1858; Henry Mitchell, born 18 November 1860; T. B., Reuben Burch, Jr., James Tillman, born 25 December 1866; and Walter Trotter, born 19 September 1872) to Hustburg, Humphreys County, Tennessee isn't known. The story of T. B.'s oldest brother, William Nicholas Loggins, that is in the Lake County, Tennessee

History Book on page 123 said that the family moved to Hustburg January 1880. (Alex Leech, grandson of W. N. Loggins who wrote the article shared the draft of the article with me at the 1992 Loggins Family reunion that was held at my mother's house in Dyer, Tennessee. Dr. James Alexander Leech was elected in 1982 for a four-year term as the first Madison County, Tennessee Executive and was re-elected in 1986 1990 1994 1998 and retired as county mayor in 2002.)Page 133 of The Trotter Genealogy by Mrs. Isham Patten Trotter, Jr. (copyright 1948) also gave January 1, 1880 as the moving date. [The information for the Trotter Family Genealogy was supplied by Reuben Burch Loggins, of Texas.] The family was listed in the 1880 District 3, Humphreys County Census. They may have actually moved a bit earlier than 1880 for on 9 January 1878 R. B. and M. E. sold a very large tact of land to R.B.'s nephews, Devotie and T. M. Billingsley. (Deed Book A, Montgomery County, Mississippi.)

The why they moved from Mississippi to Hustburg is easy to answer. T.B.'s maternal grandparents were living in Hustburg. Mitchell and Nancy Tucker McCauley Trotter had moved from Montgomery County, Tennessee where Mary Elizabeth had been born, to the Big Bottom in Humphreys County circa 1854. Mitchell and Mary Elizabeth's maternal uncle, Matthew McCauley, were large property owners. Mitchell operated a landing on the Tennessee that bore his name as late as 1983, Trotter's landing. Mitchell Trotter served as a Tennessee State Senator from 1875-1877. Mary Elizabeth had gone to visit her father's brother and her Trotter cousins in Lodi, Mississippi around the time of the family's move. According to the Trotter Genealogy, it was in the home of her cousin, Isham Patton Trotter, that she met the young widower, Reuben Burch Loggins, who had been the husband of I. P. Trotter's wife's sister.

T. B.'s Grandmother Trotter, who lived very close to them, died June 1, 1881 when T. B. was 17. She was buried in the Ebenezer Methodist Church Cemetery in Hustburg, Tennessee. (Mitchell and Nancy were Methodist. At this writing I haven't located the Ebenezer Church records but Mitchell Trotter's obituary stated that he was Methodist. Four of the six Loggins brothers were Methodist Episcopal). T. B.'s grandfather Trotter remarried in 1883 and moved to Arkadelphia, Arkansas where he died 11 January 1891. He was buried in Arkadelphia next to his second wife. [There is no stone, but there are surviving newspaper articles in the Arkadelphia Archives in the Abstracts for the Southern Standard 16 January 1891 for Mitchell and August 7, 1896 for 2nd wife, M.K. Jones Trotter.]

As implied earlier, T. B.'s paternal family valued education. T.B.'s father and uncle, William Thomas Loggins, had both attended Howard College in Alabama in 1850. William Thomas Loggins reportedly had one of the largest libraries in Choctaw County. According to the WPA Montgomery county article, his Aunt Susannah had also been sent to Alabama to attend school. (T.B.'s father, R. B., had been born in Tuscaloosa, Alabama.) T. B.'s oldest brother, William Nicholas, had attended the University of Mississippi before the family left Lodi. In addition, T.B.'s maternal family also valued education. During the year 1859 or 1860 in the Big Bottom community of Hustburg either in or near the Ebenezer Methodist Episcopal South Church was the Ebenezer Male and Female Academy that had been incorporated by the Thirty-third General Assembly of the state of Tennessee in 1859-1860. Mitchell Trotter's name was listed first on the official record that was on p. 264 of Public Acts Passed by the State of Tennessee Past at the First Session of the Thirty-third General Assembly for the years 1859-1860. Following Mitchell Trotter in the list of "body politic and corporate" were T.B.'s Aunt Angelina Trotter Parrish's husband, Nicholas C. Parrish, and T. B.'s Grandmother Nancy T. McCauley Trotter's brother, Mathew McCauley. The incorporation allowed for ninety-nine years. In the 1 June 1860 District 3, Humphreys County Federal Census, Mitchell and Nancy Trotter were boarding a teacher. The Ebenezer school was again mentioned in the 1886 Goodspeed of Humphreys County and then circa 1890's in the biography of Senator Hattie Wyatt Caraway.

T. B. may have attended the Ebenezer school in preparation for attending a Normal school. Western Kentucky University Archive records list that T. B. graduated from Glasgow Normal School in Barren, Kentucky (according to their on line records) in 1886 with an A. B. degree. He was twenty-four. He may have already been teaching for a 4 August 1937 article from the Edgewood School vertical file in the Tennessee State Archives says "in 1885...T. B. Loggins who had been teaching in the Big Bottom over in Humphreys County..."

T. B. held an A. M. Degree from National Normal University in Lebanon, Ohio according to Harold W. Stephens in his paper "The Mathematics Department 1912-1973, a Brief History, pp. 1-2. (source:http://www.memphis.edu/msci/news/documents/brief-history.pdf) Robert Ewing Corlew in his book A History of Dickson County Tennessee, 1956 pp. 160-161 states "*Loggins was a Mississippi native and a graduate of the Glasgow (Kentucky) Normal College. He did additional work at the National Normal University. The latter school conferred upon both Wade and Loggins honorary Master of Arts degrees as an award for their distinct contribution to education in Dickson County."*

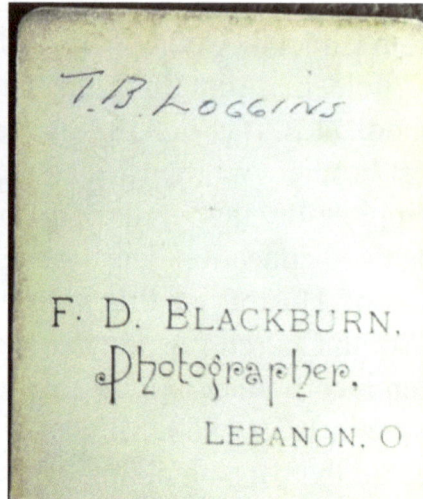

In 1884 or before, T. B. was most likely acquainted with Professor W. T. Wade who was teaching at the McAdow Seminary, a Cumberland Presbyterian School, in Waverly, Tennessee for at the start of the 1886 School year, T. B. joined Prof. Wade who had now moved to Edgewood, Tennessee as a teacher at the Edgewood Normal School on Yellow Creek in Dickson County, Tennessee. *[The picture of the young T. B. Loggins that was photographed by F. D. Blackburn of Lebanon, Ohio was shared by Beth Loggins Roberts, granddaughter of T.B.'s brother Reuben Burch Loggins, Jr.]*

National Normal was the same institution from which W. T. Wade earned his degree: "**W. T. Wade**, *B.A. '82, Dickson, Tenn. Principal of Normal College*" on page 100 of "A Roster of the Alumni and Alumnæ of the National Normal University, Lebanon, Ohio" Lebanon, Ohio, Alumnal Association, 1893-
(http://www.rootsweb.ancestry.com/~ohwarren/Places/nnu_w.htm)

As T. B. was starting his teaching assignment at Edgewood Normal School, his brother William Nicholas was running for Sheriff of Humphreys County. *""W. N. Loggins of Corn City, Big Bottom authorizes us to announce him as a candidate for Sheriff of Humphreys County Election First Thursday of August next."* The Humphreys County News July 1886 [Paper on

Microfilm at Tennessee State Archives.] There are no records that show W. N. was elected. On 29 December 1887, W. N. married a local Humphreys County girl, Sarah C. "Kate" Luten. T. B. Loggins served as the bondsman for the wedding. The couple moved to Lake County, Tennessee where they reared a large family of six girls and one boy.

[The undated picture of W. N. Loggins is from p,149 of Lake County History in Newsprint and Pictures. The photo was supplied by W.N.'s grandson, Alex Leech.]

EDGEWOOD NORMAL SCHOOL YEARS

". The main building was a large two-story wood frame structure of American classical design, with a large round turret reaching skyward, and a narrow porch at the front entrance supported by tall imposing columns. The first floor consisted of a large auditorium with a stage in one corner and two utility rooms. The upper story consisted of a large classroom plus several small rooms used to house female students. The Edgewood Normal school when completed was acclaimed as an attractive, though not beautiful structure. It was solidly constructed with spacious windows and a monument to the building skill of Capt. Will Adams. A separate dining hall was built nearby." [Nesbitt, William J. THE PRIMAL FAMILIES OF YELLOW CREEK VALLEY, 1985 THE ADVENT OF EDGEWOOD-Chapter 26] According to the District 11, Dickson County Tax record for 1887, W. T. Wade paid taxes on four acres. By 1889, the school property covered five acres. The 1890 Tax records give the property a value of $2,000.

Robert Ewing Corlew, in A History of Dickson County Tennessee, 1956, pages 160-161 discussed Edgewood Normal. *"Many people moved into the community for the purposes of educating their children. The chief feature of attraction appeared to be Professors Wade and Loggins."*

According to William J. Nesbitt in THE PRIMAL FAMILIES OF YELLOW CREEK, T. B. Loggins joined the faculty of Edgewood Normal at the start of the second school year in 1886.

> *"Other early faculty members were Professors Ike Tubbs, S. E. Hunt, Harry Hooper, Ida Stone, and Ida Foster, et all. A school year consisted of four terms, and students ranged in age from seven to adulthood. The primary department was concerned with the teaching of reading, spelling, writing, and primary arithmetic. For the older, more advance students, courses in elementary teaching, general and natural science, and the classics were offered. Instrumental and vocal music courses were also available. The school band, consisting of about twenty-five musicians, added greatly to the enrichment and enjoyment of school and social functions in the neighborhood."*

Nesbitt states that under Wade and Loggins the school began to flourish and grow.

Ruth Eleazer wrote in <u>Schools in Dickson County, Tennessee Over the Years,</u> 1986 on pages 21 through 25, that Edgewood Normal was located on Yellow Creek near Ruskin Cave. She went into length outlining the curriculum for the school. Ruth's mother was Nora Faustina Larkins. Faustina was born 12 January 1870 in Dickson County, Tennessee. Faustina and her sister Milbiria, born 5 September 1874, trained as school teachers. Both were single teachers living at home with their parents, H. J. and Elizabeth Frances Corlew Larkins in the District 6, Dickson County Federal Census. Of interest is that Ruth's grandfather, H. J. Larkins, served as the first Clerk of Dickson County, Tennessee. Although, I have found no actual record of their attendance at Edgewood, Ruth commented in the article that *"For the Natural Science Courses, the students were taken on field trips. My mother loved geology and in later years would pick up an unusual rock and tell us the name of it."* There is a record of Faustina's and Milbira's attendance at Dickson Normal College. They were included in the report of the June 1904 Institute submitted by T. B. Loggins on page 117 on the Annual Report of the State Superintendent : "Larkins, Faustina, Dickson, Co., Charlotte; and Larkins, Milbria, Dickson County, Charlotte. Faustina married V. J. Eleazor March 5, 1905 when she was thirty-five. Ruth was their first born in 1906.

Here is Ruth's comprehensive Course outline for Edgewood Normal. [Prepare to be mind boggled!]

The school year was divided into four terms, each term being approximately three months.

The courses of study in the Primary Department consisted of teaching McGuffey's New Revised Readers through McGuffey's Four, McGuffey's New Revised speller, slate and blackboard work, and Primary Arithmetic.

The Intermediate Department taught Orthography [spelling], Reading, English Grammar, Letter Writing, Geography, Third Arithmetic and Elementary Algebra.

The Elementary Department offered the teacher's course of one year which consisted of studies and drills as follows.

First Term-Advanced Arithmetic, Primary Algebra, Geography, English Grammar, Reading, Penmanship, Letter Writing, and Debating.

Second Term-Advanced Arithmetic, Advanced Algebra, United States

Third Term-Advanced Algebra, United States History, Rhetoric, Physics, Penmanship, Music, and Public Speaking.

Fourth Term-Plane Geometry, Physology [sic: Physiology], Rhetoric (Advanced), Physical Geography, Parliamentary Law,   Music, Debating and Public Finals at the close.

You took this course in one year and if you passed, you were qualified to teach. After completing the teacher's course, the scientific course of one year followed, consisting of

First Term-Solid Geometry, Beginning Latin, Geology, English Literature, Essays and Orations, Parliamentary Drill and Debating.

Second Term-Trigonometry, Caesar, Chemistry, English Literature, Essays and Orations and Debating.

Third Term-Analytical Geometry, Virgil, Physics and Zoology, English Literature, Essays and Orations, and Debating.

Fourth Term-Calculus, Sallust [a Roman historian], botany, Physiology, English Literature, Debating, Parliamentary Law and Graduation Theses.

The highest course offered was the Classic Course.

First Term-Psychotgy [sic], Cicero, Preliminary Greek lessons and Xenophon [Greek author]. Literature, Debating, and Orations and Ancient History.

Second Term-Horace, Homer, Logic, Literature, Debating and Orations and Ancient History.

Third Term- Lerry[sic: Livy], Eschylus [sic: Aeschylus], Ethics and Constitutional Government, Literature, debating and Orations and Parliamentary Law.

Fourth Term-Tacitus [ancient historian], Thucydides [ancient historian], Political Economy, Literature, Debating and Orations, and Parliamentary Law.

Instrumental and Vocal Music, the Brass Band, Art Department, Commercial and penmanship, Elocution and Physical Culture were also taught.

The students were taken on trips to visit the Ruskin Cooperative Association, or socialist colony, which was in full swing at that time.
[Note: Ruskin Cave was on Yellow Creek. Tennessee Home Locator, com lists the mileage from the town of Edgewood to Ruskin Cave as 1.4 miles NNW.]
The students living nearby walked or rode mules and horses to school, while the others boarded in the dormitory. All pupils took their meals in the large dining hall.

March 17, 1889, the Loggins boys lost their mother. Mary Elizabeth Trotter Loggins died in Hustburg. She was buried next to her mother in the Ebenezer Methodist Church Cemetery. The boys and their father erected an imposing marker to preserve her memory. [photo by Gwen. In 2015 the cedar tree fell and took off the top urn.

On 26 June 1889, according to Beth Loggins Roberts application for DAR membership, T. B. Loggins married Addie Campbell. I have found no information about Addie's training as a school teacher or when she actually began teaching at Edgewood. She was a member of the Edgewood faculty for the year 1889 for she and T. B. are both listed in the National Education Associations Tennessee Membership list for the year ending 1 July 1890. She was listed as "Loggins, Mrs. Addie C." She was listed

with an A. M. degree in the 1897-1898 Dickson Normal School Catalogue.*[picture from the collection of Henry Mitchell Loggins's family in the possession of Gwen. The same copy was in the collection of the Will Nicholas family in Tiptonville. by Thuss, 230 N.Cherry St., Nashville, Tenn].*

There is little doubt that T.B. knew Addie Campbell long before their wedding date. Addie was born on April 1, 1864 in Lodi, Choctaw County, Mississippi. On the 1870 census both T.B. and Addie are listed in Township 19 of Choctaw County, Mississippi with their respective parents. T.B.'s paternal grandparents and Addie's parents are buried in adjoining rows in the Mulberry Baptist Church Cemetery in Lodi, Mississippi.

An article in the TIMES JOURNAL of Thursday, June 12, 1890 records, "*Prof. Loggins left Edgewood Friday morning for Mississippi to spend his vacation at the home of his wife's relatives.*" Two days later on the 14th of June, Beth Campbell Loggins, T. B.'s and Addie's only child, was born in Montgomery County, Mississippi. [*Beth Campbell Loggins picture from the collection R.B. and Zula Loggins' granddaughter, Beth Loggins Rogers.*]

The Edgewood school year ending in June 1890 was well documented in the June 12, 1890 TIMES JOURNAL of Waverly, Tennessee that is on microfilm in the Tennessee State Archives.

Times Journal; Sloan & Jones-Prop's; Waverly, Tenn.
GONE HOME; FACULTY, STUDENTS AND VISITORS LEAVE EDGEWOOD WELL SATISFIED WITH THE EXERCISES.
Friday morning dawned clear and bright on beautiful little Edgewood, the scene which we are to write about, and it was a busy one on this day, and it was midnight before quiet was restored. The occasion was the returning home of students and their friends and the parting from teachers, classmates and acquaintances were touching to witness. Saturday came and went, and Sunday morning saw the village deserted by the last student visitor.

Fully 3,000 people visited the exercises, and to say they were a success would be putting it very tamely. the writer is unable to do the professors and students justice, as those who were in attendance can and will testify, that it was beyond description, and the credit due the noble founder of this institution, Prof. W. T. Wade, and his associates during the life of the school, can never be too great. Our acquaintance with him for a number of years and his most estimable lady, has been a very pleasant one, one that can never be forgotten, and it has placed us in a position to closer observe the work and success of this great institution of learning. Prof. Wade has associated with him a young gentleman from this county whose present is great, and whose future in educational work, will give its lasting impressions, as each scholastic year closes to the world and stamp him as a great instructor.---we mean Pro. W. T. Loggins. [sic: T. B. Loggins]. And while speaking of the faculty we must not forget Prof. H. T. Hooper, though in a different branch of learning to the other gentlemen---music and art--he too has taught his students knowledge which will secure for them a position in the ranks of this branch of study, as his exposition of their work testified in his class room. It is hardly just to select one student's work for especial attention, but as the picture was dedicated to the 'phat editor' of the JOURNAL, it is hoped pardon will be granted by all. It is a pen drawing of a cricket riding a little chick to water, finely executed by Mr. Geo. McCauley, of Erin, Tenn. Another very fine pen drawing worthy of note was a deer and two hounds, the work of J. J. McKelvey, of Milan, both of the professor's class.

The class in music and voice culture was in charge of Miss Katie Schollenberger, of Nashville. This little lady is a thorough teacher and a part of her class, **Miss Zula Winstead**, *Miss Annie Truby, and Ada Foster, furnished the music for the Normal class programme [sic] at their exercises. The selections played by her pupils were of a high order, and reflected credit on both pupil and teacher, among them that was most noticeable were 'The Mariner,' 'Robert le Diable,' and 'Dear Heart,' which was sung beautifully by the young lady herself. Miss Schollenberger possesses a sweet voice that is very musical and pleasing to the ear, with fine range.*

The orations delivered by the Normal class Wednesday afternoon were delivered in good style and warmly received by the audience of over 700 people, and far exceeded the expectations of their teachers and Principal, who were more than well pleased, of which we publish a summary elsewhere.

In the evening the Scientific and Classic classes held the boards, and their orations which we publish in full, held the audience for over two hours, and a more orderly and attentive audience it has never been our pleasure to be among. Every member of this class acquitted themselves nobly, to the

---

PROGRAMME.

INVOCATION. Rev. HENRY CROCKETT

VOCAL TRIO, "The Mariner," [Randegger]

BROOM DRILL,

DIALOGUE, "Which Will He Marry,"

MUSIC, "Return of Spring," Brass Quartette

UNDER THE LAURELS,

A DRAMA IN FIVE ACTS, WITH CAST

MRS. MILFORD.	BELLE SUGG
Rose Milford,	Ida Tomlinson
Polly Dowler,	Leora Heard
Sooky Button,	Carrie Balthrop
Kyle, ("Ky.") Brantford,	S. A. Myatt
Frank Colewood,	R. B. Loggins
Ike Hopper,	J. R. Heard
Bob Button,	H. A. Williams
Zeke	D. T. Gould
Sheriff	E. G. Davis

MUSIC, Grand March, ("Montello") [Pettee]

HOTEL TROUBLES, (A Farce)

TABLEAU, "Liberty and her Handmaideus." "Religion and Knowledge."

SHAKING QUAKERS,

SOLO, Cavatina, "Robert le Diable," Zula Winstead.

DRESS REFORM (A Convention.)

MUSIC, "Village Chimes," Brass Quartette

MISCHIEVOUS NEGRO, (A Farce)

TABLEAUX, (Flowers)

SOLO, "Dear Heart" Katie Schollenberger

WE ARE ALL TEETOTLERS, (A Farce)

MUSIC, "Click, Click," (Galop) [Ripley]

READING OF REVIEW, J. E. Tubb, Local Editor

MUSIC, Millie Waltzes, [Pettee]

VALEDICTORY, President

SONG, "God be With You 'Till We Meet Again." Choir

"Going Home Faculty, Students and Visitors leave Edgewood Well Satisfied with Exercises" from Waverly, Tenn. Times Journal, Thursday, June 12, 1890

credit and satisfaction of both Prof. Loggins and the Principal and audience, and each one at the close of their orations were applauded in a manner which showed the appreciation of those present.

Thursday afternoon was devoted to the exposition of the work of the students of the Geological, Botanical, Zoological and Art classes. Then followed the Philosophy class in an experimental exhibition that was amusing and entertaining; after which a drill in physics, both classes being under the supervision of Prof. Loggins.

During the afternoon Thursday, a reunion was held by the visiting students, of which there were quite a number. It consisted of talks by the students of the past, present, and future, and a general good time was had.

Thursday night the following programme [sic] was presented by the Pythagorian Literary Society of the Edgewood Normal: [see picture above]

At 8 o'clock the large hall was packed and numbers were unable to get inside to witness the entertainment which was one of the best performances that Edgewood has ever given to the public. It is estimated that 800 people were within the walls. The programme [was] carried out to the letter, and if the 'phat editor' had as many dollars in his pocket as there were laughs from the audience that night, he would certainly be able to buy his darling wife a handsome silk dress.

The orchestra music was furnished by Prof. H. t. Hooper and members of his music class assisted by the Messrs. Colwells, and Mr. Morris, of Dickson county.

NOTES

The brass band discoursed some nice music during the exercises.

Lemonade stands were in full blast during the commencement.

Goodbyes were mingled with many tears among the departing students. The lingering thoughts will ever be, the goodbye at Edgewood.

Dr. Slayden will remain at Edgewood, Tenn.

We are under lasting obligations to Mr. Hunt. Dr. Balthrop and others for favors extended.

There is a possibility of a Confederated reunion at Edgewood next year.

The success of Edgewood next year will exceed any former year.

The generosity of Mr. Thompson, Mr. Adams & Harned, and Mr. Hunt was pretty well taxed and all responded most kindly for which we feel satisfied the professors, and visitors ought to feel grateful

Catalogues for the next scholastic year are printed and will be sent out immediately. One of the most deserving subjects worthy of special notice and comment at the closing of the school, was the valedictory by Mr. Eugene Attkisson. We can not find words of praise sufficient to do this young man justice it was a masterly production one that will ever be remembered by those who heard it.

Parties desiring catalogues will please address, by postal card, Dr. W. H. Balthrop, Edgewood, Tenn.

Extra papers with the proceedings of the Edgewood exercises can be hap [sic] at 5 cts apiece postage paid by writing the publishers.

Several lots were sold by Mr. Hunt to parties Wednesday last, and several buildings will be erected immediately.

Prof. Wade was taken sick Wed. last and left Sunday in company with his wife for Virginia.

The 12 June 1890 issue of the Times Journal published the complete orations of the following students of the Scientific or Classic Classes: *"Homeward Bound" by Miss Belle Sugg; "Footsteps Echoing Through the Corridors of Time" by Miss Ida Tomlinson; "Through Labor to Rest, Through Combat to Victory" by Miss Carrie Balthrop; "Progress of the Ages" by Eugene Atkisson; "Immigration" by Elihu G. Davis; "The New South" by G. N. Springer of the Classic Class;* ***"Our Nobel Selves" by R. B. Loggins of the Classic Class;*** *"The Land of Montezuma" by W. T. Primm of the Normal Class; "Vanished Races" by Albert B. Merville of the Normal Class; "Gather Ye Rosebuds While you May" by B. F. Walker of the Normal Class; "Is Our Civilization Doomed" by Julius H. Bayer of the Normal Class;* ***"The Sky is a Roof of But One Family, I will be a Citizen of the World" by W. T. Loggins.***

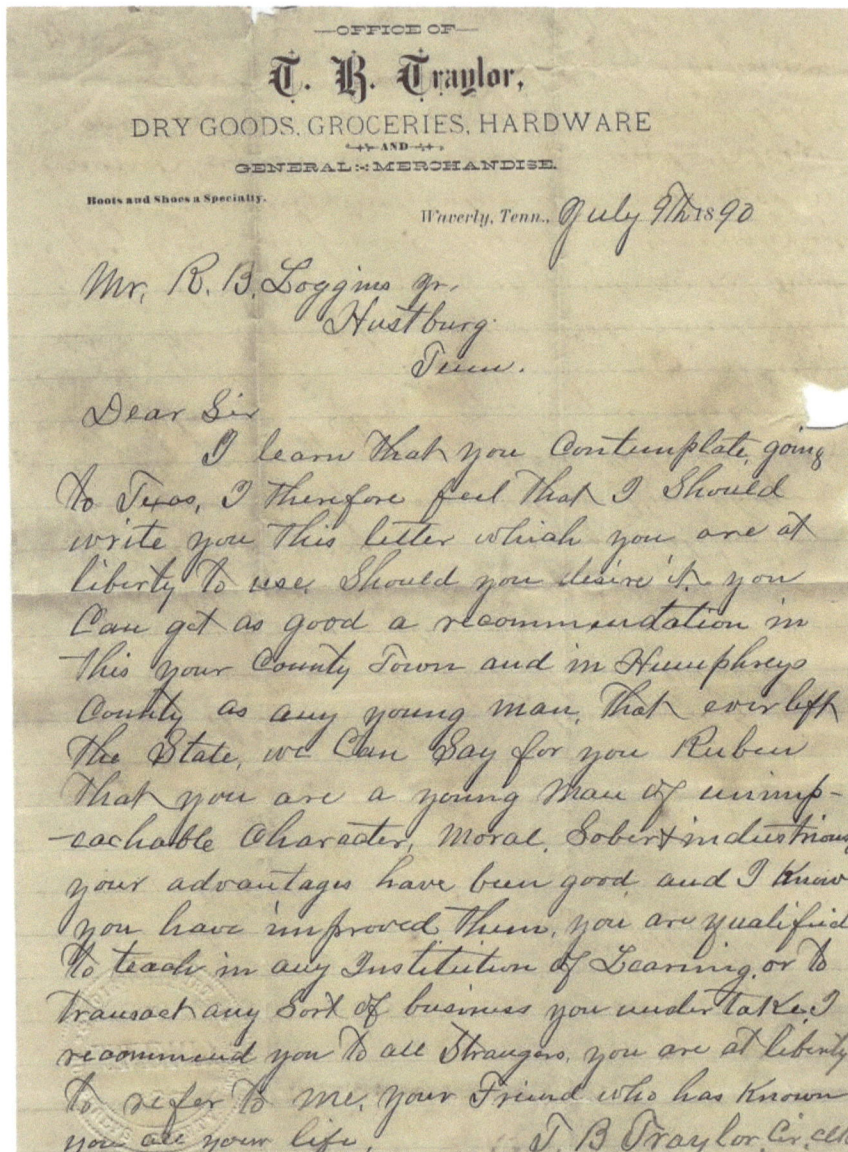

In the class of June 1890 were T. B.'s brother, Reuben Burch Loggins, Jr., and R. B.'s future bride Zula Winstead. Zula who was born and reared in Columbia, Texas was quoted in an article published in the June 12, 1947 FREEPORT FACTS that was published in Brazoria County, Texas, as saying that *"she was permitted to attend one of the best private normal schools, located at Edgewood, under the supervision of Prof. Wade, and T. B. Loggins."*

R.B. Loggins went to Brazoria County, Texas to teach after graduation. He left with a reference letter from T. B. Taylor who was serving as a Judge of the Humphreys County Circuit Court.

[Letter with Judge R. B. Loggins' Columbia, Texas descendants]

R. B. and Zula married in Columbia, Texas on January 14, 1891. By 1893 he was serving as the Superintendent of the Bellview Schools and Principal of the High School. By 1898 he had become a lawyer. He served as the County attorney and as a judge. Some of the artifacts from his life are preserved in the Brazoria County Historical and the Columbia Historical Museums.

A GROUP FROM EDGEWOOD NORMAL

The above picture is from the collection of Reuben Burch, Jr. and Zula Winstead Loggins that was shared by their granddaughter Beth Loggins Roberts. The group picture has T. B. Loggins standing on the far right next to the young woman. An article in the 4 August 1937 THE TENNESSEE GAZETTE of Nashville, Tennessee (Tennessee State Archives, Vertical File, Edgewood Normal) that was about Edgewood Normal stated that Miss Wade and Mrs. Loggins were both members of the faculty. Might the woman standing next to T. B. be Addie Campbell Loggins and the young man behind them, one of T. B.'s brothers? W. T. Wade may also be pictured.

The following pictures are from Reuben Burch and Zula Winstead Loggins' Collection of Edgewood Normal Pictures. Zula identified the pictures at the top as Walter Loggins. Water would have been about14 when T. B. began teaching at Edgewood and about 18 when T.B. moved to Dickson Normal. Zula wrote "Edgewood Friends" on the one with three men. The woman had no identification but it appears to have been taken at the same time as the older Walter Loggins picture. [Shared by Beth Loggins Roberts, R. B. and Zula's granddaughter.]

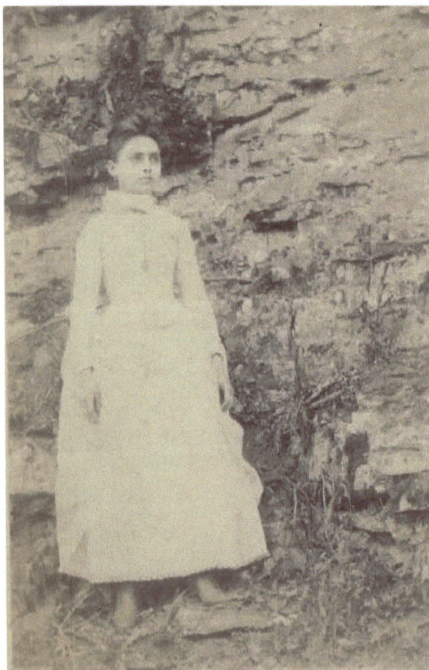

Ruth Eleazor in her section on Edgewood Normal School in <u>Schools in Dickson County, Tennessee Over the Years</u> describes the fashions: "*The fashions for the ladies at this period or the era were tight fitting basque and the long flowing skirts. They wore long hair. The men wore short hair, broad brimmed hats and quite a few wore a moustache.*"

Another photograph in Reuben Burch and Zula Winstead Loggins' collection is of Dr. W. H. Balthrop.

The following paragraph from the 12 June Humphreys County TIMES JOURNAL article about the 1890 Edgewood graduation explained his connection to Edgewood Normal.

"*Dr. Balthrop, one of the college board, and one of the most accommodating and courteous gentlemen in Dickson county, had his generosity taxed to the utmost point during the exercises. Fully 800 people were fed gratuitously by the doctor, besides a number of head of stock. This seems to us to be expecting too much from this gentleman, and to feed this number every year would eat up his profits, but as long as he does not kick there is no necessity for our doing so. He has a fine farm and raises all the meat, vegetables, etc., consumed in his large boarding hall, and will erect a fine storehouse, and rooms for the accommodation of students immediately. We are satisfied that all who were obligated to the doctor and his amiable wife, if they are like the writer feel very grateful for his hospitality.*"
(Dr. Balthrop married Cordelia Winstead in Humphreys County, Tennessee in 1883. Strong evidence suggests that Cordelia and Zula were first cousins.)

The 4 August 1937 article in THE TENNESSEE GAZETTE of Nashville, Tennessee about Edgewood gave the address of the 1886 Edgewood Normal School as Cave Mills, Tennessee.

[Dickson Co. Deed Book 29, p. 12, T. B. and Addie sold 4 January 1900 a piece of property in the town of Dickson to W.H. Balthrop a town lot. Beginning on Pitt Henslee's SE corner on Murrell Street ... to Pitt Henslee's NW corner on Joslin Street. The 1 June 1900 District 5 census listed W. H. Balthrop, his wife, Cordelia, and their children as living on College Street.]

On the 20th Day of March 1890, W. T. Wade and his wife, Lucia A, sold to T. B. Loggins "one half interest in a tract of land and the improvements thereon lying at Edgewood, Tenn. in the Eleventh Civil District of Dickson Co" for Twenty Seven hundred and fifty dollars. T. B. paid fifteen hundred dolls in cash. He was to pay the rest of the cost in installments. [Dickson County, Tennessee Deed Book V, pages 142-143]

CHANGES BEGINNING

Little did the writer of the 12 June 1890 paper know when he wrote, "The success of Edgewood next year will exceed any former year" that Edgewood Normal School would soon be losing Professors Wade and Loggins. About this time, the town of nearby Dickson began "courting" Wade and Loggins to move there. Dickson had the advantage of being served by the railroad. According to Nesbitt in PRIMAL FAMILIES OF YELLOW CREEK:

> Unfortunately at the zenith of their success at Edgewood, Wade and Loggins were enticed in 1891 to quit Edgewood and open a similar type school in Dickson. By this time the town of Dickson had become the center of population for the county and officials were very anxious to establish a college there. The Dickson town officials no doubt looked with envy on the flourishing little village school at Edgewood where many of their own citizens attended. The annual announcement published by Edgewood Normal emphasized the wholesome atmosphere of the Edgewood community-"...away from the vices of the city-no concerts, theaters, or grog shops to attract the youth into dissipation. There are no places for midnight carousels. It is void of the temptations and snares so prevalent in cities and towns, and which prove such a curse to students, drawing them away from Christian influences, and blighting their souls with a stain that culminates in an untimely grave."
>
> This type of propaganda probably went well with the parents but I doubt it was appealing to the students. The town of Dickson, although a small provincial community itself, did have a certain advantage over a strictly rural setting. It was located on a railroad and was experiencing growing pains. There was certainly more money available to finance a college in Dickson than at Edgewood. The great success of Professors Wade and Loggins at Edgewood

*naturally made them very attractive to the school officials in Dickson. Wade and
Loggins had started from scratch at Edgewood and were of proven ability. This
was 1891, some five years since its founding, and Edgewood Normal School was
at its zenith. The school had attained international status with approximately four
hundred students. Young men and women from twenty-three states were
represented. Wade and Loggins were greatly admired and loved by the students
and community. It is inconceivable that they, at this time, would harbor thoughts
of leaving to seek employment elsewhere. However, they became vulnerable to
the inducements offered by Dickson and they left Edgewood to take over the
fledgling Dickson Normal School in the spring of 1891.*

*There was much resentment naturally among the citizens of Yellow Creek.
The school officials in Dickson were accused with probable justification of
proselyting [sic] and unethical conduct. The resentment was directed chiefly at
Dickson, however Professors Wade and Loggins received a share of it also.
Yellow Creek citizens had spent much time, effort, and money in establishing
Edgewood Normal and it was a source of pride to them. If the school had been
floundering they could have better understood the exodus of the two most
esteemed professors, but as it was, the school was at its pinnacle of success.*

*James C. Hunt in a letter to a Dickson newspaper, accused everyone
involved in this scheme of unfair tactics and unethical conduct. The town of
Dickson did nothing illegal in enticing Wade and Loggins to leave Edgewood,
however their tactics were questionable and caused years of resentment.*

*Edgewood Normal didn't close its doors when Wade and Loggins left.
Most of the faculty remained and Professor S. Emmett Hunt and Ike Tubbs took
over the operation of the school with enthusiasm. Many of the students from
Dickson and the southern part of the county transferred to Dickson Normal.
Other students followed their ex mentors out of love and respect for them...."*

[This book is in the collection of the Dickson County Archives in   Charlotte,
Tennessee.]

Loggins, T. B. and Wade, W. T. were listed on the January 1, 1891
Tennessee Enumeration of Male Voters as residing in District 11
(Edgewood) of Dickson County. In addition, Wade and Loggins, according
to the 1891 District 11 Dickson County Tax records paid property taxes for
five acres of land valued at $2,00.00. This would be the last taxes they paid
in the Eleventh district for "W. T. Wade, Lucy A. Wade, wife of W. T.
Wade, and T. B. Loggins, wife of T. B. Loggins, Addie Loggins, sold the
Edgewood Normal property on the 21st day of July 1891 to M. V. Smith, W.
M. Adams, J. C. Hunt, Thomas Rogers, and J. C. Foster. [Dickson County Deed
Book W, pages 559-560.]

DICKSON NORMAL SCHOOL ERA
According to page 14 of the Dickson County History by Rick Hollis,
W. T. Wade and T. B. Loggins established the Dickson Normal School in

1891. There was a school in operation in Dickson before Wade and T. B. came for the 1893 Commencement Program stated that it was the Eighth Annual Commencement, "*but Wade and Loggins did for Dickson Normal College what they had done for Edgewood Normal, they brought national attention to the school and established it as an much sought after place of learning.*" [Dickson Academy, founded in 1885 by Professors Johns and Osborn was the predecessor according to Ruth Eleazor, p. 17 of her book Schools in Dickson County, Tennessee Over the Years, 1986.

The Deed for the purchase of what would be the Dickson Normal Property was signed on May 14, 1891.

Deed Book W Page 246-247

I, Mary W. Cox have this day bargained and sold and do hereby transfer and convey to W. T. Wade and T. B. Loggins for the consideration of Twelve hundred dollars Cash to me paid, the receipt of which is hereby acknowledged, the following tract of Land situated in the fifth district of Dickson County, Tennessee Beginning On a Stake in J Rickerts S. B. Line running South 32° W forty eight poles to a Stone at a bearing of South 41° W twenty one links from a large Spanish Oak pointer, and S 64½° E thirty nine and one half (39½) links from a large post Oak pointer, and N 23° W twenty seven and one half links from a Spanish Oak pointer Running S 58° E Twenty eight poles & two links to a Stone at a bearing of S 3° E Eighteen links from a Small Black Jack and S 56° W Thirteen links from a Small black Oak bush pointer, then N 33° E Sixty Six & three fifths (66⅗) poles to J Rickerts S.B. Line, thence West with this Line Thirty four (34) poles to the Beginning, Containing ten (10) acres To have and to hold the same to the said W. T. Wade and J B Loggins there heirs and assigns forever, I Covenant with the said W. T. Wade and J. B. Loggins that I am

p. 247

lawfully Seized of said Land, have a good right to convey it, and that the same is unincumbered, and that I will forever warrant and defend the title thereof, to the said W. T. Wade and J.B. Loggins there heirs and assigns forever. against the lawful claims of all persons whomsoever this the 14th day of May 1891

Mary. W. Cox.

State of Tennessee }
Dickson County } Personally appeard before me L L Wright a Notary Public of said County, the within named Mary W Cox the bargainor with whom I am personally acquainted and who acknowledgid that she executed the annexed instrument for the purposs therein expressed Given under my hand and Seal of office this 17th day of Feby 1892

L. D. Wright Notary Public

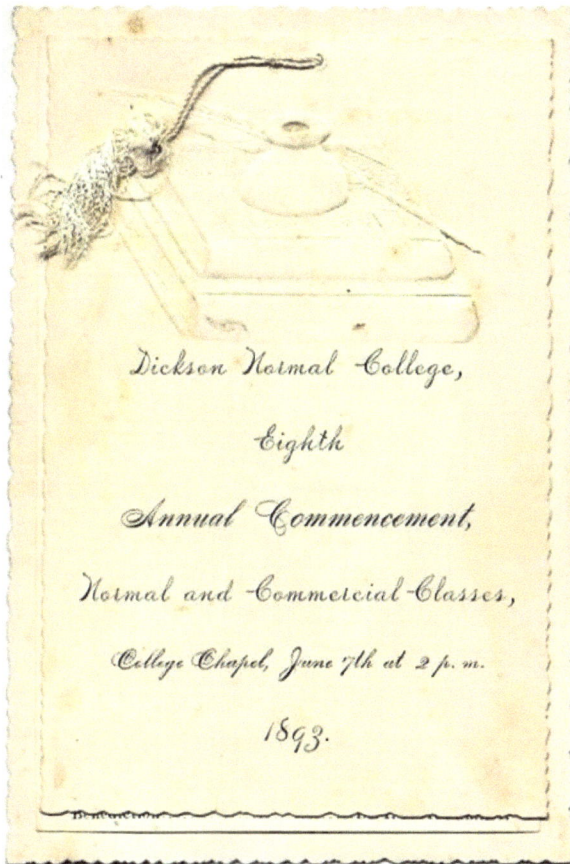

Dickson Normal College,

Eighth

Annual Commencement,

Normal and Commercial Classes,

College Chapel, June 7th at 2 p.m.

1893.

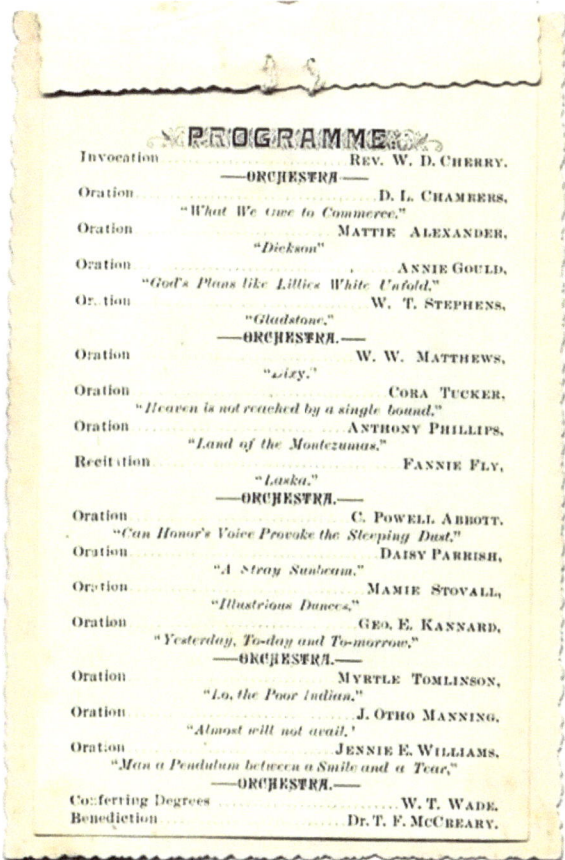

PROGRAMME

Invocation .... REV. W. D. CHERRY.
—ORCHESTRA—
Oration .... D. L. CHAMBERS,
"What We Owe to Commerce."
Oration .... MATTIE ALEXANDER,
"Dickson"
Oration .... ANNIE GOULD,
"God's Plans like Lillies White Unfold."
Oration .... W. T. STEPHENS,
"Gladstone."
—ORCHESTRA—
Oration .... W. W. MATTHEWS,
"Lizy."
Oration .... CORA TUCKER,
"Heaven is not reached by a single bound."
Oration .... ANTHONY PHILLIPS,
"Land of the Montezumas."
Recitation .... FANNIE FLY,
"Laska."
—ORCHESTRA.—
Oration .... C. POWELL ABBOTT,
"Can Honor's Voice Provoke the Sleeping Dust."
Oration .... DAISY PARRISH,
"A Stray Sunbeam."
Oration .... MAMIE STOVALL,
"Illustrious Dunces."
Oration .... GEO. E. KANNARD,
"Yesterday, To-day and To-morrow."
—ORCHESTRA.—
Oration .... MYRTLE TOMLINSON,
"Lo, the Poor Indian."
Oration .... J. OTHO MANNING,
"Almost will not avail."
Oration .... JENNIE E. WILLIAMS,
"Man a Pendulum between a Smile and a Tear."
—ORCHESTRA.—
Conferring Degrees .... W. T. WADE.
Benediction .... Dr. T. F. McCREARY.

*[Program posted to Discovering Dickson County Facebook page
11 February 2016 by Chad Bradford.]*

According to the entry for W. T. Loggins in *Who's Who in Tennessee, Memphis: Paul & Douglass Co., Publishers, 1911,* T. B.'s baby brother, Walter Trotter, graduated from Dickson Normal College at the age of nineteen in 1891. He had begun his education at Edgewood Normal. During that same year, Walter Trotter established THE CRITIC, a newspaper, in Dickson and served as its editor. The only surviving copy of the newspaper is the February 9, 1893 issue which was number Vol. 1, no. 2.

W. T. bought a lot on Rickert Avenue [Dickson Deed Book X , p. 196] near Dickson Normal College November 17, 1893 but must have resided in Dickson only a short time for in July of 1895 he was serving as the principal of the high school in Arlington, Tennessee. W. T. went on to serve, according to the Who's Who entry, as a principal in Dyersburg. He eventually settled in Somerville, Fayette County, Tennessee in the home county of his wife, Mary Jane "Jennie" Taylor Cocke whom he married 22 November 1893 in Fayette County. After his move to Fayette County, he would serve as a principal, school superintendant, and as editor and owner of the FAYETTE FALCON. I have not found written records of Jennie attending Dickson Normal College but that may have been where the two met. *[W. T. and Jennie Loggins' picture from the collection of his brother, Henry Loggins. Couple picture by Moyston, Memphis, Tenn. 338 Main St.]*

In 1892, three of the Loggins brothers were living in Dickson. T. B.'s second oldest brother, Henry, had moved from Hustburg and was living in Dickson with his wife, Tera Eola Larkins Loggins, whom he had married in Humphreys County on February 28, 1881, and their three children, Thomas Hugh, Mary, and Sammie. On August 26, 1892, Henry's son, Reuben Wilson Loggins, was born in Dickson, according to R. W.'s World War I Gibson Co, Tennessee Draft registration. The Poll tax record for 1894 lists W. T., T.B. and Henry. By 1896 Henry had moved his family to Dyer county, Tennessee before eventually settling near Yorkville in Gibson County, Tennessee. In all the census records Henry was listed as a farmer.

In this undated photograph made in Dickson, Tennessee five of the six Loggins boys were pictured. The oldest son, William Nicholas, was not in the picture. Known copies exist with the descendants of Henry, Reuben Burch, Jr. and Walter Trotter. Zula Winstead Loggins labeled her picture as follows: sitting from left to right: Tillman, Reuben, T. B. and standing left to right: Walter and Henry. The picture here is from Henry Mitchell Loggins' collection now in the possession of Gwen.

T. B.'s younger brother, James Tillman, went to Cumberland University Law School in Lebanon, Wilson County, Tennessee and graduated with a Bachelor of Law degree in the class of 1891. (Source 1892 CATALOGUE OF CUMBERLAND UNIVERSITY) Although there is no record, he probably attended Edgewood Normal before completing his education at Cumberland Law. The 1903 Cumberland University Quarterly once again gives the 1891 graduation information but also listed him as being from Waverly, Tennessee. He married Ethel McCauley on January 29, 1898 in Humphreys County, Tennessee. Ethel was the granddaughter of J. T.'s Grand Uncle Mathew McCauley. By the 1900 Census, he and Ethel were living in Justice Precinct 1, Brazoria, Texas. J.T. was practicing law. He and Ethel had no children. Eventually J. T. became a Judge. He served in the Texas Legislature from 1919-1921. J. T.'s papers are housed in the Brazoria County Museum.

36th Texas Legislature
Jan 14, 1919 - Jan 11, 1921
http://www.lrl.state.tx.us/lege Leaders/members/memberDi splay.cfm?memberID=2598

T. B.'s brother, Walter Trotter, was not the only member of the family who attended Dickson Normal school during the early 1890's. T. B.'s Grand Uncle Mathew McCauley's daughter, Alice, also attended. The following article is a little piece of "gossip" about Alice who was 16 at the time of the story. *"College Notes: Miss Alice McCauley visited her home in Hustburg, Tennessee Sunday."* 12 November 1891 DICKSON COUNTY PRESS (Microfilm-Dickson Public Library Genealogy Room, Dickson, Tennessee)
[pictured shared by Brian Soper from a picture posted by Theodore Dixon 27 Dec. 2012 to the Dixon Family Tree on Ancestry.com.]

The Dickson County Press 12 November 1891 include three separate pieces in the paper: "College Notes," "The Dickson Normal School" and a short non-titled article.

COLLEGE NOTES.

Grandmas Hopkins and Tomlinson did splendidly.

The music by the orchestra was appreciated very much.

The song by Mrs. Tucker and Miss Ogilvie was very nice.

Mr. Lieper's declamation Saturday night was superbly spoken.

Miss Alice McCauley visited her home near Huntburg Tenn., Sunday.

Miss Annie Currie deserves great praise for her success in acting the part she did.

Misses Susie Spencer and Louise Hooper visited their home near Burns last Sunday.

Misses Coffman, Woods, Lowery, Spencer, Bowman and all of the young ladies did very nicely.

Two or three of the students left for their homes Sunday. Most of them expect to come back soon.

Mr. Hughs deserves much credit for his successful management of the broom drill and his impersonification of "Eli."

Misses Bowmar and Nunn have returned to their homes for an indefinite time.

Miss Willie Cherry's dramatic taste is good. She rendered the part of a "Country Cousin" in a manner to be envied.

John Vertrees "got took in," but by a very creditable cook. Several persons we know wish they could be served as was John.

Our school is progressing rapidly and all seem to be very much pleased with it. There were forty new names enrolled Monday.

Dickson County Press 12 Nov. 1891

The Dickson Normal School.

The cheapest school in the South. For both sexes. Pre-eminently the school for the masses. Five new buildings, over fifty rooms. School furniture all new. A moral, healthy town. A full faculty of trained and experienced teachers. Board, including washing, fuel and lights, $7.00 per month. Tuition from $1.50 to $4.00. Departments, Normal, Scientific, Classic, Commercial, Musical, Type-writing, Phonography, etc. School opens August 31. For catalogue giving full information address

WADE & LOGGINS,
tf   Dickson, Tenn.

Dickson County Press for 12 November 1891

Forty new names were enrolled at the Dickson Normal College last Monday. This is the first week of the second term. This school certainly has a very bright future and Dickson is proud of it.

Dickson County Press 12 November 1891

At some point in the 1891 W. T. Wade and T. B. Loggins hired the Architecture Firm of Thompson and Gibel to design a new building for Dickson Normal School. The drawing for the school was published in the August 1893 issue of The Inland Architect and News Record. Page 11 of that issue listed the drawing under "Our Illustrations." According to The Directory of Architects, 1890, page 42, the firm of Thompson and Gibel was

located in Nashville, Tennessee in 72 and 74 of the Cole Building.
Ruth Eleazor in her <u>Schools in Dickson County, Tennessee Over the Years,</u>
1986 book states that "In 1892, the beautiful brick building was erected."
T. B. Loggins in his <u>Bulletin of Dickson College </u>that was published in the
summer of 1911 wrote the following: "*It is a private institution, the property
of its President...The property of the school consists of ten acres of land,
beautiful for situation and covered with a dense shade of native and other
trees. On this land are seven buildings, used exclusively for school purposes:
four dormitories for boys, one large hall for young ladies, one dining hall
and the main college building. The last-named was erected seventeen years
ago at a cost of more than $25,000. The grounds, buildings, and equipment
represent an outlay of more than $75,000.*"

An undated and not sourced article that was copied from one of the
Dickson County, Tennessee papers is in the vertical file of the Dickson
County Library Genealogy room. W. T. Wade and T. B. Loggins published
in the paper the architectural drawing by Thompson and Gibel along with
the following article underneath the drawing:

*To the people of Dickson County: We herewith present you with an exact likeness
of our new college building now being erected.* **We hope to have this building
ready for occupancy early in the fall** *and will use it for school purposes in
addition to the five handsome buildings erected one year ago. We feel that we
can now come before the public and offer the very best advantages for the least
money of any first class school in the country. We are spending our money, our
time, our energies and whatever talent we may have in the noble calling we have
chosen and now ask the people of the country and town to rally to us and help our
enterprise which we hope to make an honor to the people who have so liberally
given us their patronage in the past and whose patronage we hope to merit and
receive in the future. We are spending every dollar we make in forwarding the
interests of the school, erecting commodious buildings, buying new furniture and
employing able and experienced teachers. We have reduced the cost of education
all over the country. We are the pioneers in low prices. Other schools have
attempted to come to our prices and some who even one year ago ridiculed our
rates are now striving to follow in our footsteps. But we repeat we have driven
them to this and now we appeal to the people as to who is entitled to the support.
We have put education within the reach of the masses and believe the people of
our own county will show their appreciation and give us their support. You have
here in your own county the largest literary school in the state and so far as we
know in the South. No other private or normal or unendowed [sic]school south of
the Ohio River has as extensive elegant and costly buildings and grounds as the
Dickson Normal. The school has grown and prospered from the beginning. The
outlook for the future is bright. The managers hope for still greater
achievements. We do not claim all the honor to ourselves but the people of
Dickson and Dickson County claim the school. To them in a large measure is due
the success of the enterprise: to them we look for support in the future. We invite*

*all the friends of education to unite with us. You can do much. Let each friend of the school in Dickson and Dickson County send ONE student, besides his own family, no one has so little influence but he can do this. Lets all got to work and together we'll have the largest and best school in Tennessee. **Next session opens August 29th.** Board including room-rent, fuel and lights $7.00 per month, tuition from $1.50 to $4.00 per month, No school in the South offers better inducements in music, art, and elocution. Young ladies have a separate building and special care under the direct control of the principals. We shall be pleased to mail interested parties our complete catalogue on application. Thanking the people for support in the past and asking a continuation of same we are respectfully, WADE & LOGGINS, Principals, Dickson Normal College.*

A clear image of the architectural drawing is available from Ryerson and Burnham, The Art Institute of Chicago Archives Digital File #IA22XX_1315, but a payment is required to use the picture in print.: Dickson Normal College, Dickson, Tennessee, c. 1890's Thompson & Gibel,

Architects Inland Architect Collection. I have chosen to use the newspaper copy.

In Garrett, Jill Knight. Dickson County Hand Book. Easley, South Carolina: Southern Historical Press, Inc. 1984, page 284, Ms. Garrett writes under the heading Dickson Normal College: " *The brick building was demolished in 1964. It was completed by Prof W. T. Wade and Prof T. B. Loggins in the summer of 1892, following the establishment of the Dickson Normal College.* "

In the <u>River Counties</u>, November 1972 issue that was edited by Jill K. Garrett was an article "Letters from Humphreys County" that included the following on page 238. The original article was signed by W. D. Cherry and was published in the Maury Democrat, Columbia, Tenn. 10 March 1892.

"We are having some a few small schools taught here through the country. The C. P. Church Denominational School at Waverly has, I

*learn, about 150 pupils and I have been informed that old Edgewood, on the waters of Yellow Creek, has about the same number, **while Prof. W. T. Wade and T. B. Loggins have at Dickson, 44 miles from Nashville, on the N. & C. railroad, 540 pupils. I call that a booming school. Prof. Wade is a finished F. F. V., T. B. Loggins, an erudite of Big Bottom, Tenn."***

Note: F. F. V. stand for First Families of Virginia. I have made a correction in Ms. Garrett's original transcription. The original article used the word "erudite" meaning scholar.

The following Teacher's Department Dickson Normal School and Commercial Institute diploma that was issued May 7, 1892 to Faustina Larkins is Courtesy of the Ragan Family Historical Collection. W. T. Wade and Thomas B. Loggins signed as Principals and then as faculty, W.T. Wade signed as Practical Mathematics, History and Geography and T. B. Loggins signed as English and Sciences.

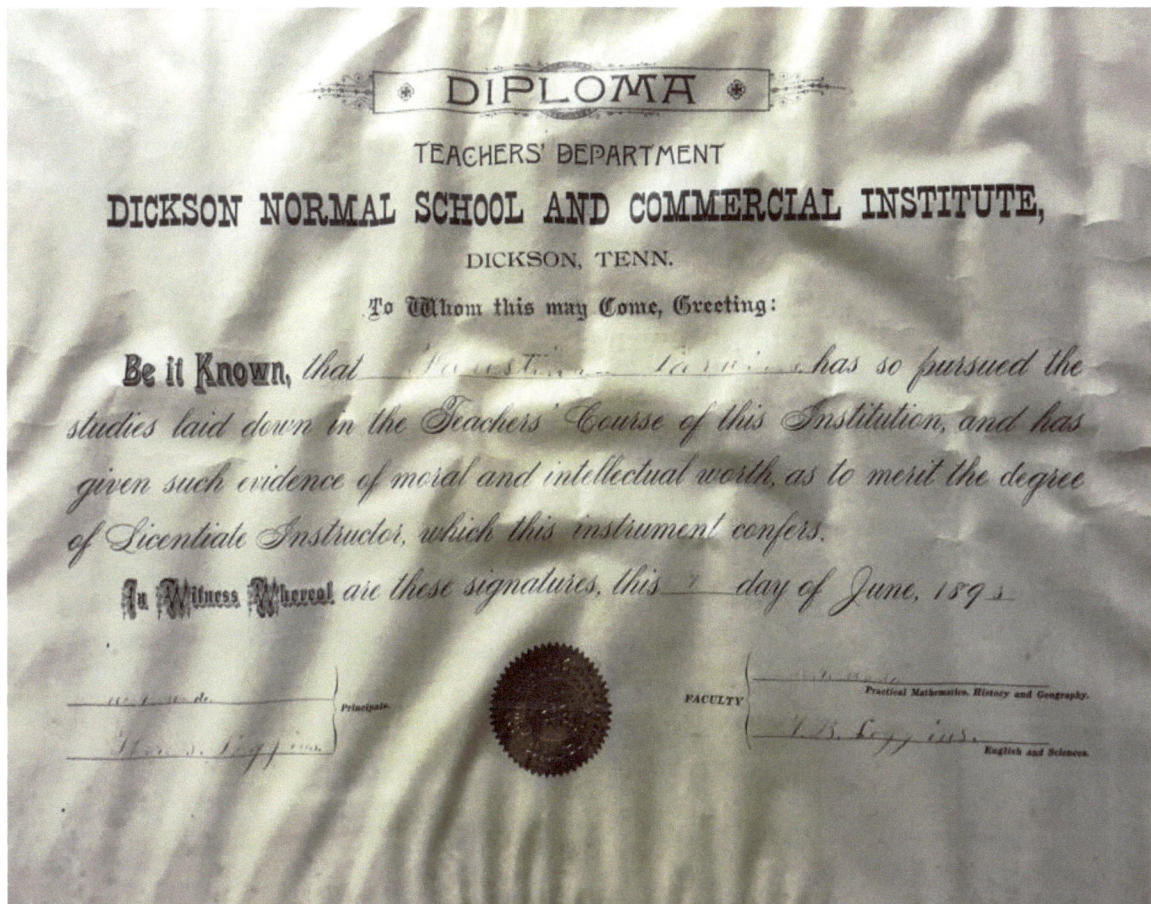

Walter Trotter Loggins devoted quite a bit of the front page of his newspaper, The Critic, Vol. 1, No. 2 that was published on Thursday,

February 9, 1893 to Dickson Normal College. The following articles were included.

THE CRITIC.

VOL. 1.   DICKSON, TENN., THURSDAY, FEBRUARY 9, 1893.   NO. 2

THE CRITIC.

W. T. LOGGINS & CO., Proprietors.

DICKSON, :: :: TENNESSEE.

Mrs. Loggins, of College Hill, has been sick for some days but is about well again now.

W. T. Loggins included the obituary of Fred Edsell. An Ancestry.com search yielded the following information about Fred. He was living in District 6, Humphreys County in the 1880 Census with his parents, William Edsell, age 51, and his mother Elizabeth Edsell, age 27. His father was a blacksmith. After Fred's death, his widowed mother remarried Anderson Choat in Humphreys County, Tennessee on 27 September 1894.

The pale horse and his rider has again visited our school and taken from our number one of our beloved school mates.

Fred Edsell was born Jan. 7th, 1872, died Feb. 2d, 1893. He embraced religion some three years before his death, and joined the M. E. Church, South, in which he lived a consistent Christian, until God saw fit in his divine wisdom to transplant him from the church militant, to the church triumphant. His illness was very brief, only four short days after the summons came. Fred had been in the Dickson Normal only a few brief months, but by his agreeable disposition and close application to his books, had won the hearts of both teachers and pupils. Although our hearts are sad and we are loth to give him up, yet we feel that "our loss is but his gain."

He was the only child of a widowed mother whom he loaves for a time, to fight her battles alone and while she will sadly miss "she mourns not as one who has no hope."

We extend to the bereaved mother and friends our sincere sympathy. And remember dear mother when God sees fit to call you from your lonely life below, that doubtless Fred "will be waiting and watching" for mother.

A SCHOOL MATE.

COLLEGE DOTS.

On the front page, 4th Column, of the February 9, 1893 edition of The Critic, W. T. Loggins included a section "College Dots" that included all of the following tidbits of College News: *Miss. Maggie Sugg has the blues of late, she will tell you why.*

Mr. Schofner, of Ripley, visited his son on College Hill last week.

Prof. W. A. Mathews of Va. will begin teaching at Centerville Monday.

Mr. Bennett of W. Tennessee, father of Miss Mary Bennett of the D. N. C. was a guest on College Hill last week.

W. W. Mathews a former student of the D. N. C. is teaching a very successful school in Hickman Co, near Aetna Furnace.

There is a very large class in Physiology this term, and they are doing some good work under the instruction of Mrs. Loggins.

There is a considerable amount of sickness in school now, and some of the students are getting scared up, but there is no danger predicted at all.

The Y. M. C. A. is doing some good work here now, and a cordial invitation is extended to the boys of the town. They meet every Sunday at 3 p. m.

We learn from the Tobacco-Leaf Chronicle of a few days ago that H. P. Gholson a former student of the D. N. C. has opened a Law office at Clarksville.

Mr. Hudson, of Gibson County, father of the well known J. G. Hudson of the D. N. C., was called here last week on account of the illness of his son; he returned on last Saturday night and carried John with him. Recent news reports him no better.

The Scientifics [sic] after following Caesar through the Gallic wars, and spanned with him the River Rhine, by a might bridge, have left him and are starting with Virgil into the war of Troy and the construction of the wooden horse. There is a large class.

The dialogue, My country cousin, was played on the stage at the D. N. C. last Saturday night, and as usual when Mr. Hughes gets blacking on his face, he brought the house to an uproar. He is a fine negro, and his brother Sam (Jack Petway) is just as good.

The instructor in the Scientific department deeming it best, has changed the way of the Scientifics and three of them spoke at the D. N. L. S. last Saturday night and all acquitted themselves very creditably. They will continue to speak from night to night till all the Scientifics and Classics have spoken.

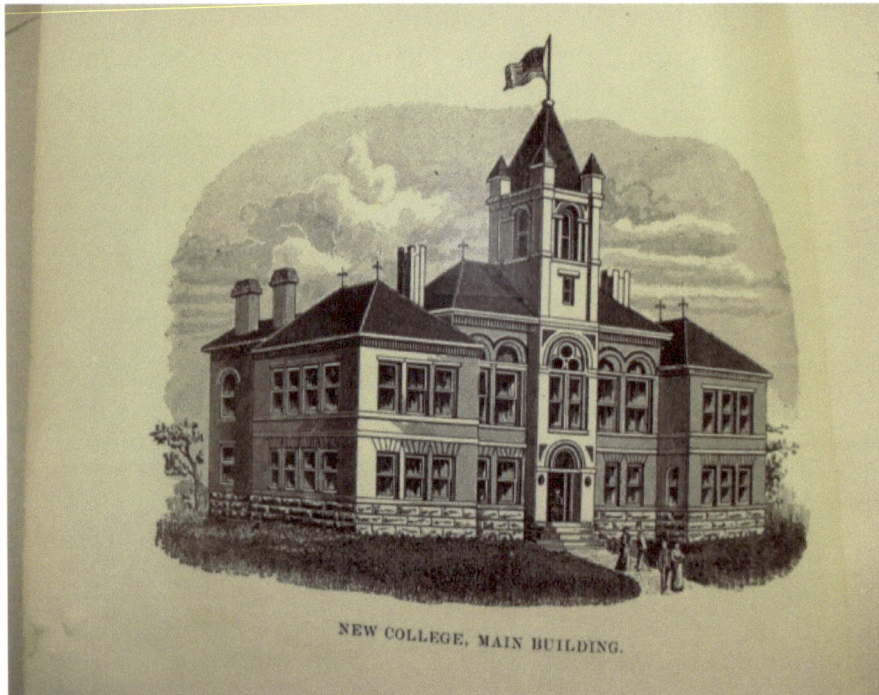

NEW COLLEGE, MAIN BUILDING.

The 1897-1898 Dickson College Catalogue refers to the building as "New College Main Building." Ms. Garrett's sheds light on why the building was called "new" in the catalogue: *"The school had been established in a frame building on what was later known as the Cox property."*

The picture of the Young Ladies Hall and Old Chapel that was included in the 1897-1898 Catalogue was of that original frame building. In addition to the two drawings, the 1897-1898 Dickson Normal College Catalogue also included a photograph that showed that the two buildings were side by side on the property. If the Ladies Hall and Chapel was one of the five buildings built by Wade and Loggins is unclear.

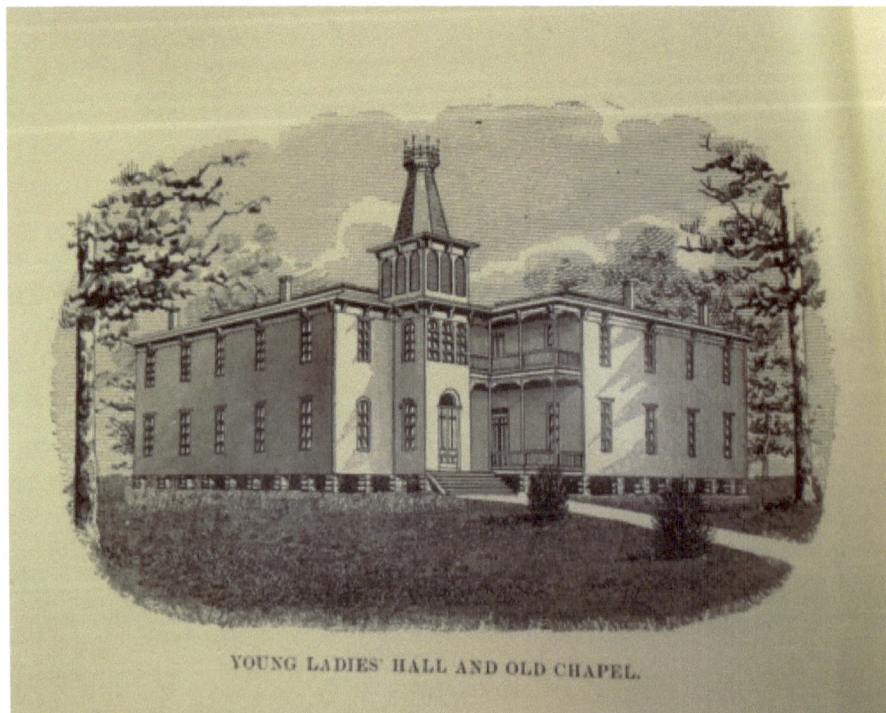

YOUNG LADIES' HALL AND OLD CHAPEL.

NEW COLLEGE.   DINING HALL, IN REAR,   OLD CHAPEL.

The Dickson County Tax Records for District 5, Dickson County, Tennessee listed that Wade and Loggins paid taxes on 10 acres valued at $5,000. Land bordered North: Rickert; South, East, West: Cox (Source: Dickson County Archives, Charlotte, Tennessee) The 1893 Dickson County District 5 Tax Records listed that Wade & Loggins paid taxes on 10 acres of land valued at $10,000. Land bordered on the North: Rickert; South: Cox; East: Dixon; West: Cox. From 1892 until 1893, the property value had doubled.

The names W. T. Wade and T. B. Loggins were inscribed above the door of the main entrance to the "New" College. (Picture from which this was made courtesy of the Ragan Family Historical Photograph Collection. They also house the Dickson Normal College 1897-1898 School Catalogue.)

Robert Ewing Corlew stated in <u>A History of Dickson County Tennessee</u>, 1956 on page 159, *"In April, 1895, one of the first teachers' institutes to be held in the county convened in Dickson for a two-day session. It was conducted by T. B. Loggins and W. T. Wade..."*

Hattie Ophelia Wyatt Caraway

Hattie's picture shared by AzKofa to Caraway Family Tree on Ancestry. com 21 Nov. 2015

Thaddeus Horatio Caraway

Thaddeus' picture shared by littlebritches102 to Rorie Family Tree on Ancestry.com 5 May 2012

In the spring of 1896, Dickson Normal School graduated a young woman who would later make history. Hattie Wyatt, who had been born in Bakersville, Humphreys County, Tennessee moved as a young girl with her parents to Hustburg, Tennessee where her father operated a store. According to program presented by John H. Whitfield in 1981 to the Humphreys County Historical Society Meeting: *"Hattie, at age 15, and her sister, Mozella, entered Dickson Normal School from which she graduated in 1896 with a B. A. Degree. While there she became engaged to Thaddeus Horatio Caraway, who had paid his way through school as a cotton picker, sawmill laborer and railway section hand. After graduation they both taught school, while he worked to obtain his law degree. In 1902 they were married and moved to Jonesboro, Arkansas."*

Additional notes by Gwen: T. H. Caraway and Hattie O. Wyatt were married 4 February 1902 by Rev. R. B. Davidson of the Methodist Episcopal South in Humphreys County, Tennessee. The two churches in District 3 at that time were Pisgah in the Plant Community and Ebenezer in Hustburg.)

Thaddeus became a United States Senator from the state of Arkansas. When he died unexpectedly during his term in office, Hattie was appointed to fill the vacancy. She went on to run for the office and was elected the first female United States Senator in 1932. She served until 1945.

This little tidbit was recorded in the <u>Nashville American</u> newspaper 13 December 1896 issue: *"Prof. T. B. Loggins, who is an applicant for State Superintendant, was in Nashville Monday and Tuesday."* There is no record of him being elected. [According to Stanford University Libraries (https://searchworks.stanford.edu/view/421676), there were no reports issued by the Tennessee State Superintendant for 1896/97-1897/98. In the Annual Report for the School Year ending June 30, 1900, the State Superintendant Morgan C. Fitzpatrick, listed that Price Thomas had served as State Superintendant from 1897-1899.]

The 1897-1898 School Catalog provided much information about Dickson Normal School in addition to the pictures of the school campus that

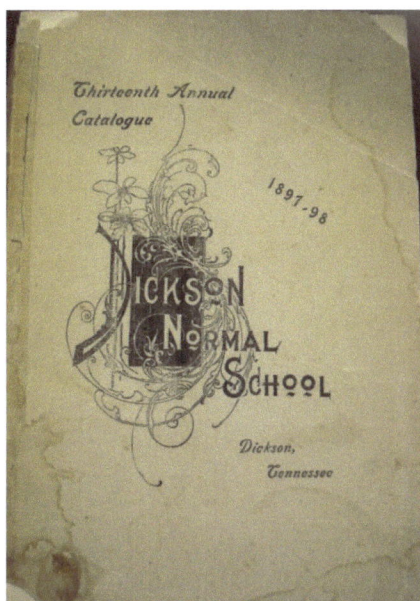

were presented earlier. The catalog also included a school calendar and the explanation of each of the courses and other information. Included on the page was this statement of purpose:

"A Normal school for the masses: Thorough, Practical, Moral, Religious, and Non-Sectarian."

W.T. Wade and T. B. Loggins also gave this guarantee on the title page of the catalog:

"We Guarantee every statement made in these pages and should any one come here and find that any thing fails to come up to our advertisement, we will either make it good, or pay traveling expenses both ways."

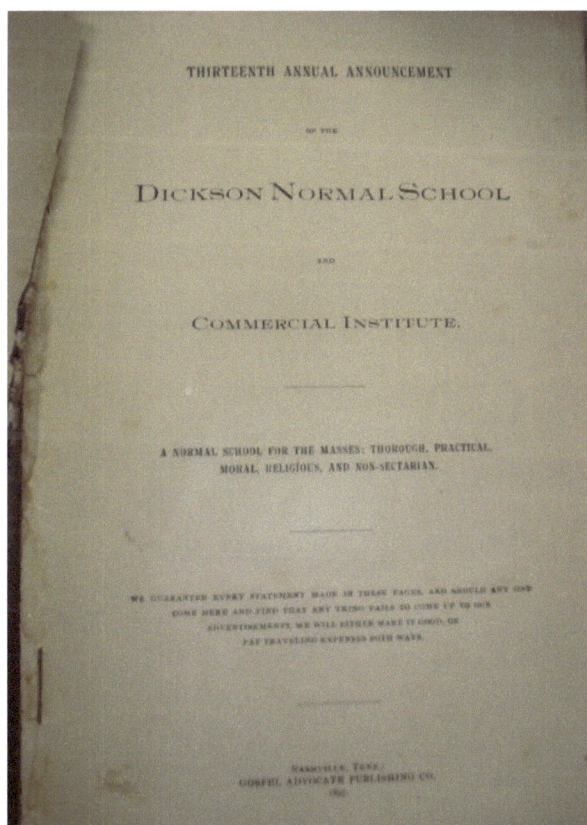

A NORMAL SCHOOL FOR THE MASSES: THOROUGH, PRACTICAL, MORAL, RELIGIOUS, NON-SECTARIAN

FACULTY.

W. T. WADE and T. B. LOGGINS,
Associate Principals.

W. T. WADE, A.M.,
Practical Mathematics, Greek, and Metaphysics.

T. B. LOGGINS, A.M.,
Advanced Latin, Sciences, and Higher Mathematics.

MRS. LUCIA A. WADE, B.S., B. Accts.,
German and Bookkeeping.

MRS. ADDIE C. LOGGINS, A.M.,
Beginning Latin and History.

MISS EMMA HART,
Elocution and English.

ALLISON C. HUGHES,
Preparatory Mathematics, History, and Geography.

PROF. J. L. WYMAN,
Pianoforte, Vocal Culture, and Director of Orchestra.

MISS MATTIE DOZIER,
Principal of Art School.

JOE DAVIS,
Penmanship and Vocal Music.

MISS JESSIE HOOPER,
Phonography and Typewriting.

MRS. MAMIE FITZHUGH,
Telegraphy.

The 1897-1898 catalogue provided a list of the faculty and what each person taught.

Faculty: *W. T. Wade and T. B. Loggins, Associate Principals; W. T. Wade, A. M, Practical Mathematics, Greek, Metaphysics; T. B. Loggins, A. M., Advanced Latin, Sciences, and Higher Mathematics; Mrs. Lucia A. Wade, B. S., B. accts, German and Bookkeeping; Mrs. Addie C. Loggins, A. M., Beginning Latin and History; Miss Emma Hart, Elocution and English; Allison C. Hughes, Preparatory Mathematics, History, Geography; Prof. J. L. Wyman, Pianoforte, Vocal Culture, and Director of Orchestra; Miss Mattie Dozier, Principal of Art School; Joe Davis, Penmanship and Vocal Music; Miss Jessie Hooper, *Phonography and Typewriting; Mrs. Mamie Fitzhugh, Telegraphy*

```
*Phonography is a method of writing in shorthand that uses
symbols to represent speech sounds
```

In the 1897-1898 Catalogue, the following topics were outlined in through detail. On page 7 "To All who are Seeking Educational Advantages:

> *"We have taken hundreds of poor boys from the plow, and poor girls from the profitless routine of the kitchen, and by helping and encouraging have placed them on the road to success. Others who had worked for years in the school room at low wages have in a few months at our school prepared themselves for higher spheres of usefulness. Some are in wholesale houses selling goods an keeping books; some are representing the largest commercial and Insurance companies in the United States; others are practicing law, practicing medicine, teaching high schools, or preaching the Gospel."*

On page 10"Why the Dickson Normal is the Best," and on page 11"Dickson An Ideal Place for a School,

> *"Dickson being situated, as it is, on the elevated rim-lands of Middle Tennessee, on the highest point between Nashville and the Mississippi River, and twenty miles from the Cumberland River, is far removed from the malarial districts of the South and West, in a region of pure air, bright skies, rolling hills, and laughing waters. For healthfulness it is unsurpassed. There are no marshes or stagnant pools of water. The streams are all clear and healthful, and send their limpid currents rushing over rocky beds, rippling as they go. From the sides of the hills cold streams of pure, sparkling water gush forth, tempting the weary traveler to stop and slake his thirst."*

According to Page 13 of the 1997-1998 Catalogue, Normal or Teachers' Course were divided into four ten week course that required a year of study.

1) Higher Arithmetic, Geography and History English Grammar, Primary Algebra, American Literature, Elocution, Letter writing. 2) Higher Arithmetic, Higher Algebra, English Grammar, Physiology, American Literature, Elocution, Debating. 3) Rhetoric, Higher Algebra, Physics, Civil Government, American Literature, Elocution, Debating. 4) Plane Geometry, Geology, Rhetoric, Physics, American Authors, Theory and Practice of Teaching

Upon successful completion of the above courses, the student received a certificate.

Page 15 of the 1887-1888 Catalogue stated that the Commercial Course could be completed in two ten week sessions:

1) Bookkeeping, Arithmetic, English Grammar, Letter-writing, Penmanship, Debating and 2) Bookkeeping, Actual Business, English Grammar, Penmanship, Business Correspondence, Debating.

Upon successful completion of the above courses, the student received a diploma.

Of the Scientific Course outlined on pages 16 -17 of the aforementioned catalogue, the professors gave the following explanation: *"This course has been arranged to meet the wants of those who are unable to take a more thorough collegiate course, and yet desire the essentials of a liberal education, or thorough preparation for any of the learned professions, or practical duties of a successful business life. This is preeminently a course in deep thought and original investigation."* The Scientific course was also designed to require a year of study with four ten-week sessions.

1) English History, Solid Geometry, Beginning Latin, Astronomy, English Literature, Elocution, Debating, Essays. 2) French History, Trigonometry, Caesar, Chemistry, English Literature, Elocution, Debating, Essays. 3) Oriental History, Analytical Geometry, Virgil, Chemistry, English Literature, Elocution, Debating, Essays, 4) Calculus, Virgil, Botany and Zoology, Current History, English Literature, Elocution, Debating, and Parliamentary Law

Upon successful completion of the above courses, the student was awarded the degree of Bachelor of Science or B. S.

To provide for students who wanted more Latin, Dickson Normal College offered a one year Special Scientific Course. The four terms for this course were outlined on page 18:

1) English History, Trigonometry, Virgil, Astronomy, Debating, Essays, Elocution. 2) French History, Analytics, Sallust, Chemistry, English Literature, Debating, Essays, Elocution 3) General History, Calculus, Sallust, Higher Rhetoric, Experiments in Chemistry, English Literature, Debating, Essays 4) General History, Higher Rhetoric, Ovid, Botany and Zoology, English Literature, Parliamentary Law, Current History, Essays.

A special note was added to this section: *"Classes in Beginning Latin will be organized every term, so no one need leave the Dickson Normal without a thorough knowledge of the language."*

The Literary and Historical Course outlined on page 19 had as its prerequisite, the Scientific Course. It took one year to complete the following four terms in the Literary and Historical Course. After the completion of this course of work the student received a Bachelor of Philosophy or PhB.

1) Sallust, Greek History, Ethics, Elocution, Debating, Essays 2) Cicero, Political Economy, Roman History, Elocution, Essays, Debating, 3) Horace, Psychology, Medieval History, Elocution, Essays, Debating 4) Tacitus, Logic, Modern History, Debating, Parliamentary Law

In this section on page 20 the following statement was made about the Literary and Historical Course: *"Essays and class lectures will be written and delivered before the class and teachers through the year, and subjected to the severest criticism. Public addresses will also be delivered by the students in this course before the entire school and the people of the town, at stated intervals or morning exercises, as the teacher may direct."* In addition the following statement suggested who would benefit from the course: *"Pupils who complete this course have an eminent qualification upon which to lay the successful basis for business or a profession--Law, Medicine, Theology, Teaching, Literature, Journalism."*

The final offering was the Classic Course. One also received the Bachelor of Philosophy degree upon successful completion.
1) Sallust, Greek or German Lessons, Ethics, Elocution, Essays and Debating, Parliamentary Law 2) Cicero, Xenophon or German, Political Economy, Elocution, Essays and Debating, Parliamentary Law. 3) Horace, Homer or German, Psychology, Elocution, Essays and Debating, Parliamentary Law 4) Tacitus, Thucydides or German, Logic, Elocution, Essays and Debating Parliamentary Law.

Page 22 discussed the Musical Department for the 1897-1898 School year that was to be headed by Prof. Jacob L. Wyman. *"He has had a successful experience of more than twenty years both in the United States and Canada."* The departments of study were Piano, Organ, Vocal Culture, Violin, Guitar, Cornet, Through Bass, Harmony, and Orchestral Work. Students could earn a certificate in music or work some music courses into their other studies. Performing was expected weekly at the Literary Society. Students gave recitals each term. The complete list of all the pieces of music to be studied was given in the course requirements.

Pages 25 - 27 discuss some of the other class offerings. Penmanship was taught by Professor Joe Davis who had earned his B.S. degree from Dickson Normal. In addition to plain penmanship, Mr. Davis offered courses in Artistic Penmanship. Miss Jessie Hooper, also a Dickson Normal student, taught Typewriting and Phonography. Miss Mamie Fitzhugh taught Telegraphy. The Art Department was under the control of Miss Dozier who was *"fresh from the poplar Art School of Boston."* She was known for her portraits.

Pages 28 -30 listed the costs of the programs. Page 28 broke down each course cost on a monthly bases. Page 30 gave the overall costs without the addition of individual music classes. The summary of Expenses for a Ten Month Year: Necessary Expenses for board, room, rent, fuel was $70.00 and for tuition the cost was from $25.00 to $50.00 depending on the course of study.

The rest of page 30 through page 47 of the booklet contains the following topics: Boarding Arrangements for Young Ladies, Special to Those of Limited Means, Why We Should Be Patronized, Unsurpassed Advantages (which includes twenty different statements including the fact that Dickson County has no saloon!), Library and Reading Room, Methods, Private Instruction, General Items, Special (which contains such items as students must furnish their own sheets and towels, keep their room neat, and "all idlers, loafers, and 'roughs' will be dismissed from the halls.") Degrees and Diplomas, Grades, Selection of Study, Cards of Patrons, Character of Our Pupils, and Geological Collections. In this catalogue was a special section on the Tennessee Centennial Celebration:

> *"This year Nashville will be the center of attraction for the whole South, on account of the Centennial that is attracting so much attention. No part of an education is more valuable than such an exhibition of our natural resources and wonderful achievements. Our nearness to Nashville and the special rates will allow any pupil to visit the Centennial, spend the whole day, and return for a mere sum This is a fact worth remembering."*

The next to the last section was "How to Reach Dickson.*"*

> *"Dickson is situated on the Nashville, Chattanooga and St. Louis Railway, at the terminus of the Clarksville Mineral and of the Nashville and Tuscaloosa Railways, forty miles west of Nashville. Any depot agent can tell you how to come, what changes you will have to make, and what it will cost. Parties living on the Tennessee River will come by boat to Johnsonville, thence by rail to Dickson. When you reach Dickson, come at once to our office. Young ladies coming alone will be met at the depot by one of the teachers, if they will let us know when they are coming.*

For Catalogue or further information address Wade & Loggins, Dickson, Tenn."

The last section in the catalogue was a complete listing of the 1896-1897 graduates with their states. Among those listed was Addie Campbell Loggins' niece, Cammie Peeples (Eliza Campbell Peeples) who was born 27 December 1876 in Webster County, Mississippi to Dabney Guilford and Eliza Barbara Campbell Peeples. Eliza Barbara was Addie's half sister. Cammie's obituary that was posted in the Winona, Mississippi <u>The Winona Times</u> on November 1, 1973 stated *" Mrs. Aldridge taught school there after attending Dickerson Normal College in Tennessee."* Cammie's cousin, Beth L. Rogers of Phoenix, Arizona was listed as a survivor. (Obituary Posted to Find a Grave Memorial #21401234.)

In addition to work, the students of Dickson Normal School participated in a number of outings. Research using the Tennessee State Archives Newspaper Data base that is available in the Reading Room provided many references to Dickson Normal School in the Middle Tennessee Papers. Two Such articles in the <u>Nashville American</u> were in the 27 April 1897 issue that talked about a picnic at Kingston Springs and in the 16 May 1898 issue about an outing to Bon Aqua.

The statistics for the 1898-1899 school year were included in the <u>Annual Reports of the Department of the Interior for the Fiscal Year Ended June 30, 1899, Report of the Commissioner of Education, Vol. 2</u>, page 1838, line 136. Dickson Normal College made the following report. The entire

number of people employed by the institution was seven males and seven females. Three males and three females were involved in instructing Normal students. The entire enrollment for the school was 300 males and 265 females. There were 183 male students and 145 female students that were listed as below Normal students and high school grades. There were 152 males students in the Normal courses and 115 female students in the Normal courses.

(The above photograph of Addie, Beth, and T. B. Loggins is from the collection of R.B. and Zula Loggins. The date of the photograph is not known. by Thuss, 230 N. Cherry St., Nashville, Tenn.)

T. B. Loggins bought two pieces of property in the town of Dickson in 1899. First, on October 23, 1899 T. B. bought a piece of property for $54.00 from N. R. Sugg and his wife, Jennie D. Sugg described as *"In the 5th Civil District Dickson County...as follows: Beginning on the south east corner of a lot sold by Dickson Lodge F &A. M. No. 468 to F. F. Tidwell on College Street running eastward by seven feet to Mary Cox line thence northward by 276 feet to Mary Cox line and thence westwardly with said Mary Cox line 127 feet to a stake on a thirty-foot street thence southwardly with thirty foot street 136 feet to a stake in the line of a tract of land sold by said Dickson Lodge F & A. M. No. 468 to N. R. Sugg and thence eastwardly with the line of the lot sold by said Dickson Lodge F. & A. M. No. 468 to the said N. R. Sugg and the line of the lot sold by said Dickson Lodge to F. F. Tidwell 120 feet thence southwardly with the said F. F. Tidwell's line 150 feet to the beginning.*(Dickson County Deeds, Book 29, page 11) Second, he bought another piece of property in the town of Dickson on November 10, 1899 for $175.00 from F. F. Tidwell and his wife, M. K. Tidwell that was described as *"bounded as follows: Beginning at Pitt Hensley's S.E. corner running "E" wardly with Murrell St. sixty feet to a stake thence northwardly one hundred & fifty feet to a stake thence westwardly sixty feet to a stake to the said Pitt Henslee north east corner thence southwardly one hundred fifty feet with said Henslee line to Murrell St. the beginning."*(Dickson County Deeds Book 29, pages 3-4)

The two undated photographs by Moore in Dickson, Tenn. were of young Beth Loggins. The picture with the dog was in R. B. and Zula Loggins' collection of photographs that is now in the possession of their descendants in Texas. The one with the coat was in Henry and Tera's collection now in the possession of Gwen.

A new teacher of Elocution was on the faculty by January 1900. *Werner's Magazine, Vol. XXIV, No. 5 for January 1900, page 354 "Miss Tommie Bell Chambers has charge of the elocution department of **Dickson Normal College**."* Miss Chambers was mentioned again in the May 1900 issue: " *Werner's Magazine, Vol. XXV, No. 3 of May, 1900, page 317 "Miss Tommie Bell Chambers was the reciter [sic]at a concert given under the auspices of the Dickson Aeolian Club, her numbers being "A Telephone Romance," "Heads Not Hearts Are Trumps," and the pantomime "Comin' thro' the Rye."*

The June, 1900 Werner's Magazine issue mentioned her on page 365: *""**Dickson Normal College** reports successful and up-to-date methods in elocution, in charge of Miss Tommie Bell Chambers."* On page 353 of the June,1900 issue was a picture of Miss Chambers with a picture of her students performing. [Note: I used my camera to take a picture of the computer screen as this was a Google Book posting.]

TOMMIE BELL CHAMBERS.
DICKSON NORMAL COLLEGE, DICKSON, TENN.
Tableau by pupils, " He passed to be with Jesus in the singing of the hymn,"
From the musical recitation, " The Last Hymn."

The statistics for the 1899-1900 are included in the <u>Annual Reports of the Department of the Interior for the Fiscal Year Ended June 30, 1900, Report of the Commissioner of Education, Vol. 2</u>, page 2114, line 113.

Dickson Normal College made the following report. The entire number of people employed by the institution was eight males and eight females. Three males and two females were involved in instructing Normal students. The entire enrollment for the school was 325 males and 250 females. There were 110 male students and 105 female students that were listed as below Normal students and high school grades. There were 190 males students in the Normal courses and 115 female students in the Normal courses.

The 1900, 5th Civil District Federal Census enumerated nine people as living at Dickson Normal College in three separate households: #139: Wade, William (Head), a teacher and Wade, Lucy A (wife), a teacher; #140: Loggins, Thomas B. (Head), a teacher and Loggins, Addie C (wife), a teacher, Loggins, Beth (daughter), at school; Campbell, John L. (father), a teacher; Davies, William (Boarder), a teacher; #141 Hughs, Allison C (Head), a teacher and Hughs, Lula (wife), a librarian. In the "Ownership of Home" section both William Wade and Thomas B. Loggins were shown as 1) owning the home, 2) free from mortgage, 3.) home not farm. [Note: John L. Campbell was Addie Campbell Loggins' father.]

1900 5th Civil District, Dickson County, Tennessee Federal Census taken by James B. Robinson on the 8th Day of June 1900. (Source: Actual Records posted on Ancestry.com.)

The Annual Report of the State Superintendant of Public Instruction for Tennessee for the Scholastic Year Ending June 30, 1902, page 77 listed the county as Dickson, the address of the President or Principal as W. T. Wade, Dickson, the number of teachers as fifteen, the number of pupils as 400, the degrees conferred as B. S. or A. B, the age of the institution as 15 years, the seating capacity as 600 and the value of the school property as $30,000.

The summer of 1904 was important in the history of Dickson Normal College. That summer, the school hosted one of the Summer Institutes for education. A total of 184 teachers participated in the Institute with 148 Primary teachers and 36 High School teachers. There were twenty different Tennessee Counties represented with thirteen from Middle Tennessee and seven from West Tennessee. Dickson county, Tennessee, as one would expect, had the highest number of teachers enrolled. Addie C. Loggins participated as a student in the Institute. At the end of the report was a full

42

list in alphabetical order of the participates and their county of residence. (See appendix for the list.) T. B. Loggins, as the conductor of the Institute made a full report to the Tennessee State Superintendent of Schools:

ANNUAL REPORT OF THE STATE SUPERINTENDENT OF PUBLIC INSTRUCTION FOR TENNESSEE FOR THE SCHOLASTIC YEAR ENDING JUNE 30, 1904, Pp. 112-119

STATE INSTITUTE, DICKSON June 6, Four Weeks

Sir--The statistical report of the Secretary, found below, will doubtless give you the information desired relative to the State Institute you so kindly located at Dickson. As Conductor of the Institute I desire, however, to make this supplemental report. I have been connected with State Institutes in Tennessee for a number of years, and I do not hesitate to say this was the most satisfactory I have ever witnessed. The work done by the large body of teachers was above the average. The entire time of the Institute was devoted to the work, and nothing allowed to interfere therewith None but bona fide teachers were enrolled, and the attendance was remarkably regular and uniform. Very few came except to work and be benefited. Many of the teachers who were in attendance had previously taken the State work and held State certificates, but all of them, as per your instructions, took the examination again, and not a single certificate was renewed or otherwise issued, save upon satisfactory examination.

It was unanimously agreed among the faculty that the State Institute examinations should be more rigid, so that State certificates would mean more than they were beginning to mean in some sections of the State. How well we succeeded in this you may see from copies of the questions used, which I herewith submit for your inspection.

Better helpers than Supt. J. B. Cummings, Supt. E. B. Wilson and Supt. W. C. Lawson were never appointed to an Institute. They are not only capable and efficient instructors, but tireless workers, who, at any sacrifice of self, were willing at all times to do anything in their power for the success of the Institute or the good of the individual teachers. I hereby express to you my thanks for furnishing such a faculty, and to them for invaluable assistance in making the Institute a success. Supt. P. L. Harned was with us two days, and delivered interesting and helpful lectures on the general status and some needed reforms in the public schools. His work was appreciated by the Institute. Miss Georgia Oliver, your special instructor in Primary methods, was with us several days and did excellent and much needed work.

In conclusion, permit me to say that the County Court, which so generously contributed to the Institute financially, and the citizens of the county and town, and especially the teachers of the county, thoroughly appreciate your continued recognition of Dickson's superb accessibility and adaptability to summer State Institute work, and thank you most cordially for locating the Institute in our midst.

Very respectfully,

T. B. Loggins, Conductor

Sir--The following report of the State Institute, conducted at Dickson, Tenn., from June 6 to July 1, 1904, is most respectfully submitted;

The most cordial feeling existed throughout the Institute not only among the individual members of the faculty, but between faculty and teachers, and also between the teachers and the citizens of the town. Dickson is an ideal place for a State Institute, and it was a common remark with the members of the Institute and visitors that no better place could have been selected in the State. The fine college buildings, and abundant shade, the inexhaustible supply of pure water, the height above sea level, the cool breezes and the ample facilities and cheap rates of board make it most acceptable to teachers.

The following work was assigned by the Conductor as soon as the faculty was announced and consulted:

T. B. Loggins__Grammar, Physiology, Agriculture, Geology, Physics
E. B. Wilson--United States History, School Management, Geometry, Pedagogy
J. B. Cummings--Tennessee History, Arithmetic, Civil Government, Bookkeeping
W. C. Lawson--Reading, Spelling, Geography, Rhetoric, Algebra.

In the series of articles that Robert S. Clement wrote for <u>The Dickson County Free Press</u> that were compiled by H. Alan Ragan into the book <u>"From Mile Post 42...To City of Dickson 1980</u>, Mr. Clement on p. 56 wrote:

"On August 4, 1904, Professor Loggins came before the Council (city of Dickson) and asked to be relieved of his taxes for 1902-1903, amounting to about $33.00, as compensation for the use of his building for public school purposes, which request was granted."

Dickson College, Dickson, Tenn.

(Courtesy of Ragan Family Historical Photograph Collection)

Robert Ewing Corlew must have had access to the 1904 32-page booklet for Dickson Normal College for on pages 162-163 of <u>A History of Dickson County Tennessee,</u> he stated that *"Professor Wade had been forced to retire to a farm in his native Virginia because of ill health."* In researching Prof. Wade after Dickson Normal, I found census records for Snow Creek, Franklin County, Virginia. Willie T. Wade was listed as a farmer. Lucy A. Wade was listed as a teacher in a Private School. Ruth Eleazor in her section on Dickson Normal College in <u>Schools in Dickson County, Tennessee Over the Years</u> wrote that Prof. Wade died in Rock Mountain, Virginia November 24, 1916. He was 68 years old. He had been born November 1848.

A report for Dickson Normal College in THE ANNUAL REPORT OF THE SUPERINTENDENT OF PUPLIC INSTRUCTION FOR TENNESSEE FOR THE YEAR ENDING JUNE 30, 1905, was not included on the table on page 86, but in PICTORIAL HISTORY OF DICKSON COUNTY, TENNESSEE 1803-2013 by the Dickson County Historical and Genealogical Society there are several pictures from the 1905 school year at Dickson Normal College on pages 212 and 214. The source of the pictures was not noted, but they were from Clara Brown's Dickson Normal Scrapbook. Clara captioned her pictures with white ink. The album is now part of the Ragan Family Historical Collection in Dickson, Tennessee and

the pictures are shared in this work thanks to the Ragan Family.

The Boarding Students' pictures were made with the white frame, Old Chapel and Girls Dorm as a backdrop. The photo below has T.B.'s location indicated with an arrow.

All the boarding students in front of the girls dormitory in 1905

In the above picture, Clara Brown marked herself with a white arrow on the top right near the pillar. T. B, marked with new arrow, is on the right standing on the ground behind the seated boys.

Arrow pointing to Clara Brown.

Thanks to Clara's caption: "Clara Brown Union City, Tennessee" I could research to determine who she was. Clara Belle Brown, according to her Tennessee Delayed Birth Certificate was born December 2, 1887 in Hornbeak, Obion County, Tennessee to Emerson Ethridge and Wince Sophronia Kendall Brown. In December 11, 1906 in Obion County, Tennessee she married Oscar T. Wilson. Clara, not only had a picture of Oscar in her scrapbook, she also had a picture of Henderson College in Henderson, Tennessee which was the school Oscar was attending. Henderson College is now known as Freed Haredman University.

The girls & teachers that boarded at the
dormitory in 1905 at Dickson Tennessee
Pro. Loggins the gentleman you see
was the president of the school

An almost "Where is Waldo" picture of T. B. Loggins among the girls who boarded in 1905 was also included in Clara's album. Another of her pictures from that year shows T. B. in the middle, seated, among another group of students.

The students from West Tennessee
Dickson 1905

Clara included a picture of the Commercial Class in her album. She also had an individual picture of the professor labeled "Prof Perdue Commercial" in her scrapbook and in another picture that will appear later in this work, Mr. R. E. Perdue was also pictured walking with a group of the female students from the college. [Reed Ellis Perdue was the son of William Wiley and Cordelia Wyatt Perdue. According to his TN Delayed Birth Certificate, he was born in Sumner Co., TN 25 April 1880. He was living with his parents in the 1900 Simpson Co., KY census. June 6, 1904 he attended the Tennessee Sate Teacher's Institute at Dickson Normal College. By 12 September 1918 he was the cashier in the Leeds State Bank in Jefferson Co., Alabama. By 1940 he was the president of a bank in Gadsden, Alabama.]

The _____ class in 1905 at Dickson Normal College. Arrow pointing to the teacher. Purdue.

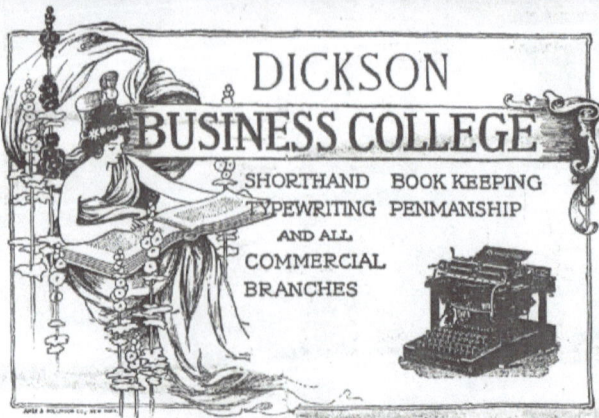

DICKSON BUSINESS COLLEGE

SHORTHAND BOOK KEEPING
TYPEWRITING PENMANSHIP
AND ALL
COMMERCIAL
BRANCHES

48

One of the true treasures from Clara Brown's scrapbook is her picture of the Dickson Normal School Faculty for 1905. Unfortunately she does not give the names of the teachers. I have been unable to locate a list of the 1905 teachers. T.B. was the second man on the front row on the right. The lady on the far right next to him may have been Addie C. Loggins. Prof. Purdue was the man at the back on the left.

According to p. 953 of The American Bar, 1921, one of the students who graduated from Dickson Normal College in 1905 with a B. S. degree was Robert Ewing Corlew who went on to attend Cumberland Law School in Lebanon, Tennessee. He served as the Superintendent of Dickson County

Schools in 1903, 1904, and 1907. He was the father of the author of <u>A History of Dickson County Tennessee, 1956</u>. In the book <u>Dickson County, Tennessee 1803-2003 Two Hundred Years of Family</u>, the article "Robert E. Corlew, Sr. Father of Public Education in Dickson County December 25, 1873-January 29, 1930 is the following paragraph:

> *"Bob Corlew received much encouragement from two able school men who came into Dickson County in the 1880's, Professors W. T. Wade of Virginia and T. B. Loggins. The first established a school called 'Edgewood' in the Yellow Creek Community and announced that they could train young people who could read and write to become teachers after just one year of schooling at their school. After a few years in the Yellow Creek Community, they responded to the demand for their services by moving their school to Dickson, where they founded the 'Dickson Normal College.'"*

This paragraph implies that Mr. Corlew took the courses necessary to receive his Teacher's Certificate at Edgewood Normal but then later decided that he would continue his education and pursue a degree at Dickson Normal College.

There is much documentation for the Summer Institute that T. B. Loggins conducted in Obion County, Tennessee from July 5th to July 1st in 1905. In addition to the public record that was sent to the State Superintendent of Education for the State of Tennessee, there is also a personal letter that T. B. wrote to his brother, Will Loggins, during the institute. Will gave the letter to T. B.'s and Will's brother, Henry. The letter is now in the possession of Gwen, Henry's great granddaughter. (picture circa 1905, Henry and Family)

First is the newsy note that T. B. wrote to the family on June 7, 1905 at the beginning of the Institute. There were basically three parts to the letter. The first part appears to be concerning Will's need to find a good teacher for a school in Lake County. The second part concerned family matters. The third part was about a young woman named Mosie Wyatt and her job as a teacher. Mosie Wyatt, Humphreys County was on the list of Institute participants for the 1904 Summer Institute at Dickson Normal College.

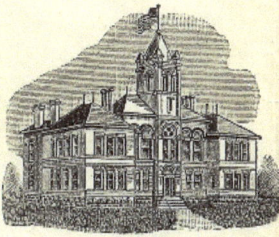

Dickson Normal College.

T. B. LOGGINS, Principal.

Dickson, Tenn. June 7-1905.

My dear Bro. Will:-

Your letter came, I was indeed glad to hear from you. I looked carefully over my list but found only one man who was out of a position who would make you an ideal man and he had partially made trade and had to wait, Unless you have heard from him by this time he too cannot accept, I would not recommend a man unless I knew him, If you have not a man yet write J. W. Blair, Wilcox Bldg. Nashville Tenn, and tell him just what kind of man you want and tell him I asked you to write him, He has an agency and is thoroughly reliable, Addie and Beth were so anxious to come with me and to visit you but Addie was not able when I left home, She hopes to come yet. I will go home Friday eve and come back Sunday, She will come the next week if she's strong enough and stay one week with you and one with Henry. We are all anxious to come over, I hope to come o

myself for Saturday and Sunday. Addie is not
very well and we have to husband her strength
all we can. As soon as she is able she will
come and we shall all see you. Give our
love to Kate and the children,

We are having a very large and a very
prosperous Institute. We have 250
teachers here now and will run to 300.
Maxie Logan asked me to get you to
see her Directors and get them to decide
what they would do about her proposition
and for you to wire her. She wants to
come back to the Institute next week if
she teaches, If not she wants to stay with her
mother. She will have to enter Institute
next Monday to get a certificate as
the law requires 15 days. Write me. Hoping
to see you while I am over here and with love
for all I am your Bro

T. B. Loggins.

Dickson Normal College/T.B. Loggins, Principal Obion, Tenn/ June 7, 1905 My dear Bro. Will: Your letter came. I was indeed glad to hear from you. I looked carefully over my list but only one man who was out of a position who would make you an ideal man and he had partially made trade and had to wait. Unless, you have heard from him by this time he too cannot accept. I would not recommend a man unless I knew him. If you have not a man yet write J. W. Blair, Wilcox Bld, Nashville, Tenn and tell him just what kind of man you want and tell him I asked you to write him.

Addie and Beth are so anxious to come with me and to visit you but Addie was not able when I left home. She hopes to come yet. I will go home Friday eve and come back Sunday. She will come the next week if she's strong enough and stay one week with you and one with Henry. We are anxious to come over. I hope to come over myself for Saturday and Sunday. Addie is not very well and we have to conserve her strength all we can. As soon as she is able she will come and we shall all see you. Give our love to Kate and the children. [note: excellent rail service in 1905]

*We are having a very large and a very prosperous institute. We have 250 teachers here now and will run to 300. *Mosie Wyatt asked me to get you to see her Directors and get them to decide what they would do about her position and for you to wire her. She wants to come back to the institute next week if she teaches. If not she wants to stay with her mother. She will have to enter Institute next Monday to get a certificate or the (*can't make out*) 15 days. Write me. Hoping to see you while I'm over here with love for all I am your Bro   T. B. Loggins*

*Note: Mosie B. Wyat must have found out from Will Loggins that her directors had rehired her, for in the <u>Bulletin of The Dickson Normal School, June/July 1905</u>, she was listed in the section "Grades Made By Pupils of Dickson Normal College in the State Institute, Secondary Course, Four-year Certificate Good Anywhere in Tennessee." Her grades were Geology-99, Physics-97, Bookkeeping-95, Algebra-100, Civil Government-96, Geometry-90, Psychology-97, Rhetoric-98, Agriculture-95.

Mozella Bell Wyatt was two years older than her famous sister, Hattie Ophelia Wyatt. Mosie had grown up in Hustburg, too. From the tone of the letter, we may assume that both Will and T. B. were well acquainted with the family. Mosie married John Shell Abbott in Humphreys County 10 January 1906. They moved to Oklahoma where he stayed. She had moved to Newbern, Tennessee by the 1920 Census. Her son and mother were living with her. By 1 April 1930 she was a clerk in the Library of Congress in Washington, D. C. Mosie died in 1941 and was buried in the Fairview Cemetery in Dyersburg, Tennessee.

The official report for the 1905 Summer Institute in Obion, Obion County, Tennessee did not list all the participants. In addition to the report by T. B. Loggins and the Secretary of the Institute, there were also two separate resolutions, one from the town and one from the pupils.

Annual Report of the State Superintendent of Public Education for Tennessee for the Scholastic Year Ending June 30, 1905. pages 112-115:
STATE INSTITUTE, OBION June 5 to July 1, 1905

Sir--The people of the good town of Obion were a unit in their endeavors to do all possible for the success of the institute and for the convenience, comfort, entertainment and pleasure of the members of the institute and faculty. I have never known a town where and institute was located to strive so hard or succeed so well in royally entertaining it. They cared for, and through their well chosen committees, handled the nearly 400 teachers who were there with ease, system and success.

The institute was largely attended. Indeed, it was too large for best results. Of the nearly 400 teachers who enrolled, many of them were young, too young to make successful teachers, and in some instances, to comprehend the work. While this is true, we had many mature, well trained and experienced teachers who did excellent work, and who will have an influence for good in the schools of the State.

The faculty selected by you were able and efficient workers, and were in thorough accord with the conductor in and endeavor to give rigid examinations, and require a higher standard for State certificates. Much is due them for the success of the institute. We desire to thank you for sending to our institute Superintendent P. L. Harned and Miss Mattie Butler. Superintendent Harned's lectures were practical and helpful. Miss Butler did excellent work for the primary teachers.

The institute thoroughly enjoyed the addresses delivered by Senator Carmack, Gen. H. H. Hannah, Congressman F. J. Garrett and the Hon. Joseph E. Washington.

My experience in this and other institutes leads me to make the following recommendations:

First--That if possible there should be more uniformity in both the examination questions and in the grading of papers for State institutes.

Second--Owing to the fact that so many boys and girls too young to teach and manage schools are rushing into State institutes that an age limitation be prescribed for teachers.

Third--That applicants be allowed only two years after the completion of the primary course for the secondary work, taking at least half of it each year. Respectfully,
T. B. Loggins

Faculty and Division of Work
T. B. Loggins, Conductor--English Grammar, Physiology, Geology, Agriculture
B. F. Watson, Secretary--U. S. History, Rhetoric, Pedagogy
J. B. Cummings--Tennessee History, Arithmetic, and Bookkeeping
R. E. L. Bynum--Geography, Geometry, Civil Government
J. M. Moore--Physics, Algebra, Reading Spelling

An excerpt from the town resolution reads: "Resolved, By the citizens of Obion, that we hereby tender our sincere thanks ...second, for appointing such a competent, painstaking and efficient worker as Prof. T. B. Loggins, Conductor..."

The student resolution is as follows: "Be it resolved, By the pupils of the Obion Institute, that we extend to our conductor, Prof. T. B. Loggins, our hearty and sincere thanks for the able manner in which he has conducted this institute, and also tender the other instructors our appreciation for the efficient help they have given us in our studies.
Passed unanimously by the institute.

In the Vertical File of the Dickson County Public Library Genealogy Room is a copy of the <u>Bulletin of Dickson Normal, Vol. 2, No.1, June/July 1905.</u> The original was obviously printed on newsprint. The pages measure 91/2 inches by 14 inches. The first page has a picture of the "Main Building-Front View" and at the bottom lists T. B. Loggins, Principal. The courses of study were outlined but "The Course in Detail" broke the Curriculum into six broad categories with sub divisions within each. 1)Mathematics: Arithmetic, Algebra 2) Higher Mathematics: Geometry, Trigonometry, Analytical Geometry 3) Grammar: Grammar, Rhetoric, History 4) Natural Sciences: Chemistry, Natural Philosophy, Botany, Geology. There were Five Departments with the exact material studied in each department: Department of English, Ancient Languages, School of Elocution and Oratory that was taught by Miss Nell Porch, Music Department that was headed by Prof. D. L. Swank who offered piano, organ, voice, mandolin, violin, and guitar. In the *"Examinations"* section, the names and grades were given of those DNC students who took part in the Summer Institutes. In the *"To Our Pupils"* section the author of the text in the paper was made clear, when all sentences were begun with "Write me," "Give me," and "Send me." The section *"What They Say About Us"* contained letters from various educators and clergy. The *"In the D. N. C. and Who Have Taken the State Examinations Say of Us"* quotes the following students: D. T. Barnhill of Carroll County, Mollie Sandburg of Obion County, Joe Pickle of Weakley County, Ruby Coppedge of Stewart County, R. H. Bone of Obion County, Charles L. Baldridge of Obion County, Gertrude Rogers of Shelby County, A. S. Norvell of Gibson County, R. E. Gorham of Stewart County, Ada Bone, Ella Nicholson of Gibson County, Amanda Few of Dickson County, Delia Taylor of Crockett County, A. W. Harkey of Weakley County, a Taylor of Weakley County, and Sallie Summers of Stewart County. Two pages were devoted to *"Dickson Business College."* There were five photographs in addition to the drawing of the Young Ladies hall and the cover photograph: Part of Obion Delegation, Boarding Pupils from Dickson,

Our Home County, Actual Scene in our Commercial College--Pupils at Work, Professor Swank and Part of His Music Class, D. N. C.'s Baseball Team and D. N. C's Football Team. Sadly, the photocopies make identifying the people in the photographs too difficult. (Clara Brown included in her 1905 Scrapbook a picture of Professor Swank and his music class and the 1905 Dickson Normal Football teams.)

Clara is pictured with a group of girls that she dated February 16, 1906.

Feb. 16 - 1906   W.N.C.

Ella Ketzone   Lillie Mae Cavender   Myrtle Snow   Bess Underwood   Onnie Petty   Ethel Turner   Camille Fleming   Leona Brown   Brightmore

The section "Improvements on College Hill" gave information about some of the work that had been and was to be done to the buildings as well as a little advertising:

> "Our four large dormitories for young men, situated on the college campus and facing Normal avenue, have been newly and neatly repaired and painted. They are in first-class condition and furnish to our young men a neat and comfortable residence than can be found anywhere. The material is on site to put the Young Ladies' Hall in new and thorough repair. The building will be ceiled and painted throughout to correspond with the rest of College Hill. The shade trees and grassy lawns surrounding these buildings together with the purest and best of Middle Tennessee water from a deep well (one hundred and twenty-five feet in depth) and five well-kept cisterns, make ideal accommodations for those who wish to study. Surely College Hill is a 'thing of beauty and a joy forever.'"

[Note: T. B. identifies a street as Normal Avenue, but there is no street by that name in the 1900, 1910 or 1920 Dickson Censuses, nor was there an Academy St. as there is in 2016. There is record of Academy Avenue in the 1937 City Records. (Clement, p. 181)]

T. B. Loggins, in his "State Institute" Section wrote "*At this writing (the close of the first week) ....It is a special privilege to the principal of the school, who is also conductor of the institute to be thrown again with these splendid young men and women.*" The end of the first week would have been Friday, June 9th.

In the series of articles that Robert S. Clement wrote for The Dickson County Free Press that were compiled by H. Alan Ragan into the book "From Mile Post 42...To City of Dickson 1980, Mr. Clement wrote on page 38 of the book that he had gone to school at the Dickson Normal College as a first grader beginning in 1906. "*I remember quite well my first day in school because part of the plaster in the ceiling fell and I wondered if this happened everyday. Fortunately only one was injured.*"

In 1906 on page 532 the GEOGRAPHICAL DICTIONARY OF THE WORLD had this listing: "*Dickson, a banking post-town of Dickson Co., Tenn., on the Nashville, Chattanooga and St. Louis R., 42 miles W. of Nashville. It has manufactures of staves, handles, lumber, etc., and it is the seat of Dickson Normal College. Pop. in 1900, 1363.*"

THE ANNUAL REPORT OF THE SUPERINTENDENT OF PUBLIC INSTRUCTION FOR THE STATE OF TENNESSEE FOR THE YEAR ENDING JUNE 30, 1906. pp. gives the following information about Dickson Normal College: County: Dickson; President or Principal: T. B. Loggins; Town: Dickson. No other information listed for the College.

In 1906, T. B. Loggins participated as a member of the faculty for the Summer Institute that was held in Dickson County, Tennessee June 4, 1906 to June 15, 1906. The conductor of the Institute, W. A. White, gave very little information in his report. He did state that T. B. Loggins taught Grammar and Physiology. (Source, page 304 of The Annual Report of the Superintendent of Puplic Education for Tennessee for the Scholastic Year Ending June 30, 1906.) There was no mention of exactly where the Institute was held in Dickson County.

Of interest in the aforementioned report on page 302 was that T. B.'s brother, W. T. Loggins, taught in the Summer Institute that had been held in Decatur County, Tennessee July 2, 1906 to July 6, 1906. W. T. Loggins taught Grammar, Arithmetic, Physiology, and United States History.

In 1907, T. B. Loggins was a member of the Religious Education Association. He was listed on page 368 under Tennessee as "Loggins, T. B., A. M., President Dickson Normal College" in the 1907 publication The Materials of Religious Education.

In The Taylor-Trotwood Magazine, Volume 4, March, 1907 edited by Robert Love Taylor, John Trotwood Moore, Thornwell Jacobs on page 677, T. B. and Dickson Normal College are mentioned in a story, "Dickson County, Tennessee," by W. O. Thomas.

"Dickson is the chief commercial town in Dickson county. Charlotte is the county seat, but it has a population of only a few hundred. The population of Dickson numbers about three thousand. Within five years it has almost doubled its inhabitants. It has a chancery and circuit court and a larger and costlier courthouse than the county seat. Being accessible by three railroads, it is the logical commercial and political center of the county. It is also the educational center. In addition to a good public school system, it is the seat of the Dickson Normal College. This is a co-education institution. The college building is modern and commodious in its every appointment. It is situated in a beautiful grove of native oaks, on a broad table land overlooking the town of Dickson. A corps of trained teachers is in charge of the work. The curriculum embraces a four-years' course, beginning with an exhaustive study of the common school branches and including a comprehensive course in language, science and mathematics. T. B. Loggins, A. M., is the principal of the college. The enrollment includes students of both sexes from all parts of the state.

Undated Photograph of Dickson Normal College. (Courtesy of the Ragan Family Historical Photograph Collection.)

An announcement in the June 7, 1907 <u>Tennessee Republican</u> that was published in Huntington, Carroll County, Tennessee stated "*The State Teachers' Institute of West Tennessee will open in McKenzie.. T. B. Loggins will be conductor assisted by W. R. Richardson of Huntington, J. B. Cummins and H. E. Watters.*" (Source: Transcription by Anita Emberlin.) http://www.gamilytreemaker.genealogy.com/forum/regional/states/topics/tn/30185/)

Dickson Business College

DESERVES YOUR SUPPORT

BECAUSE

It is best in location.
Most complete in equipment.
Latest in courses and methods.
Most practical and progressive.
Most thorough in teaching.
Highest in standards.
Most economical.
Best in results because it educates for life.

Our Specialties:

Bookkeeping, Shorthand, Typewriting, Telegraphy, Penmanship, Arithmetic, and English Correspondence.

Our Motto:

The highest business training for our young people and a good position for every one who completes our courses.

Enter any time. Address

T. B. LOGGINS,
Dickson, Tenn.

In the <u>The Annual Report of the Superintendent of Public Education for Tennessee for the Scholastic Year Ending June 30, 1907,</u> page 88 on a chart that lists private schools, T. B. Loggins was listed as the President or Principal of Dickson College. The report stated that there were 16 teachers and 700 total pupils with 500 from Tennessee between the ages of 6 and twenty-one. The school was twenty-three years old and the school property was worth $75,000. Dickson College, according to the chart, was maintained by some public funding.

The Dickson County Herald, 12 December 1907 issue carried the following "Notes from the College" column.

Thanksgiving was greatly enjoyed at College. The pupils need and enjoyed the rest.

The address by Miss Davis, of Atlanta, Ga, on Mission, was the best ever heard in the town on the subject.

Rev. W. H. Wright of Humphreys County visited his daughter Emma at College Saturday and Sunday.

Mrs. P. A. Sowell, of Nashville, Miss Davies, of Atlanta, Ga., Rev. and Mrs. D. E. Hinkle and Miss Ettie Spicer, Dickson, took Thanksgiving dinner at the College.

Mr. Coleman Williams, one of the best citizens of Dickson visited his daughter, Miss Emma, who is a member of the Senior Class.

A number of the Teachers and pupils went to Burns Saturday to the Dickson County Teachers' Institute. A great dinner and a good time at Burns for those who attended.

Quite a number have endorsed the note last week asking for a ten Months' public school Do you? If you do, talk it and especially speak to the Town Council. It is the one thing needed to make Dickson take its proper place among the towns of the State. We are losing more citizens yearly from this than all other causes.

No more Lyceum numbers till Jan. 1st, unless the classes in Music and Elocution give an entertainment or the Juniors give that night with Robert Burns, it is going to seem long between times to those who like to be entertained.

Prof. P. Edwards, teacher of Book-keeping, Short-hand and Telegraphy, in the College, spent Sunday and Monday with home folks in Western Ky. He is back at his post now and is the most popular Commercial teacher the school has had.

Things are getting lively around the College Office now. New matter is being sent out. Within two weeks 8 or 10 thousand pieces of mail will go out. A large increase of students is expected with the beginning of the new year.

Rev. D. E. Hinkle has organized a class in Mission study, at the college. The class meets Monday at 2:30 P. M. It is interdenominational and has to do with the study of Missions only. The first book to be studied is "Uplift of China." Quite a large circle has started on the work.

Work is being done on the buildings. Fuel is being put in place and College Hill will soon have the appearance of being ready for winter.

Everett Melton, one of the good boys of the school and of the town has been confined at home from sickness. We are glad to have him visit us this week. In a week more he will be back in his place in the classes.

The entire school is now being given lessons free in vocal music by Prof Swank the able music teacher of the College, and in Physical Culture, by Miss Barrett, the efficient teacher of Expression. The work is doing much good and is greatly enjoyed.

Miss Ida Reynolds, the Hall teacher reports 66 perfect in chapel deportment this month, as against 53 last month. Twenty one out of the Twenty-three Seniors were on this Honor Roll.

Senior class: Hal Bernard, Fred A. Coon, George Collins, Willie E. Dickerson, Andy Eggstein, Tennie Easley, Percy Freeman, Frank Frazier, Webb Goodlett, Beth Loggins, Doy Myatt, Porter E. Odom. Phinous Rodgers, S. M. Rutledge, J. A. Rainbolt, Harris Sheeley, Marvin Springer, Claud Stroud, Ethel Wilson, Emma Williams.
Junior Class--E. O. Anderson, Annie Beauchamp, Emerald Chandler, W. B. Lunsford, W. R. Liming, Carrie Moore, Wilson Petty, Annie Lou Reeves, S. H. Snow, Rosie Shore, Fannie Webb, Florence Perry.
Sophomores--Myrtle Andrews, Gayle Balthrop, Lizzie Bowen, Fannie Crosby, Ernest Chew, Floyd Chew, Marcellus Dewy, Lucy Holt, Annie Payne, Lillie Petway, Rose Rickert, T. K. Shappley, Clayton Smith.
Freshman Class: Jno Anderson, Sarah Andrews, L. C. Buttrey, Editeh Badge, Mabel Beasley, Katie Bargie (not sure of spelling), Bertha Crosby, Ethel Easley, Louise Freeman, Buchannan Grigsby, Kate Grisby, Archie Hood, Sara Herington, Lula b. Hopkins, Ouida Smith, Nannie Swift, Delmar Tidwell, Emma Thomas, Flandy Taylor.
Not one of these young people has so much as spoken once in the chapel for a month.

New classes in all branches will be added for those who want to teach. The new term will begin Tuesday, Jan. 14th.

The Dickson County Herald, 20 December 1907 issue carried the following "School Notes" column.

Six of the Senior class are from Louisiana, ten from Dickson, and fourteen from other parts in the county.

The senior class will deliver their finals for the first half of the year on Nov. 19 and (2?), at 7:30 p. m. The program is two parts on account of the number of the class. All are invited There will be no admission fee.

This is the best year in the history of the Dickson College. This is true whether we measure the school by numbers or by the qualities of its students. There are twenty-three in the Senior class. The Junior, Sophomore, and Freshmen classes are all large and strong.

R. B. Hearn of Carroll county, Lonnie Gibbons of Shelby county and Frank Sellers of Obion county entered this week. Messers Hearn and Sellers are in the Commercial department. Miss Whitaker entered the Junior Class and Matte Gibbons the Freshman.

The Senior class organized electing Frank Frasier of Dickson President. Willie Dickson of White Bluff Secretary.

The Junior class elected Alex English of Dickson President and Dockey Ship of Dickson Secretary.

The Sophomores elected Virgil Massey of Carroll county President and Homer Avery of Crocket county Secretary. The Freshmen will organize soon.

The second <u>Bulletin of Dickson Normal College</u> in the Vertical Files in the Genealogy Room of the Dickson County Public Library is not dated, but "Term Begins on January 14, 1908" implies that the bulletin was published at the end of 1907. This issue had much the same format as the 1905 issue. The front cover is the same. The Dickson Commercial College section describes the Bookkeeping, Complete Bookkeeping, Shorter Bookkeeping, Shorthand, Typewriting and Telegraphy courses in detail. Dickson College had also added the "Department of Civil Service, or Training for Government Positions" because *"the government needs hundreds of young people for civil-service positions."* The "State Institute Department" section told what was the same and what courses had been added. The Bulletin also contained letters of recommendation for the college and for President T. B. Loggins by **Seymour A. Mynders**, Superintendent of Knoxville City Schools; **M.E. Doran**, Department of Public Instruction, Williamson County; **Fred J. Page**, County

Superintendent; **Norman M. Byars**, Clerk and Master, Haywood County, Brownsville, Tenn. (who mentions he was a former student); **Wicliffe Rose**, Dean Peabody College; **R. S. Boyers**, Caldwell, Texas; **R. J. Wood**, Pastor of Baptist Church in Dickson; **William H. Johnston**, Presiding Elder of Dickson District, Tennessee Conference.

Information about the upper class officers was given. The Senior Class of 1908 had elected the following officers: **Frank Frazier**, president and **Miss Willie Dickerson**, secretary. The executive committee for the class was **Hal Bernard**, **Doy Myatt**, **Emma Williams**, **L. L. Wood**, and **Beth Loggins** (T. B.'s daughter). The Junior Class of 1909 officers were **Alex English**, president and *Miss **Dockie Shipp**. [*discussed later in this work.]The Sophomore Class of 1910 elected **Virgil Massey**, president, and **Homer Avery**, secretary. There were pictures of each of the classes. In addition there was a picture of the Study Hall and an "Actual Scene in Our Commercial College-Pupils at Work."

Clara Brown's captions for her 1905 pictures: "*The same study hall with the faculty assembled on the stage.*"

Removed to increase the size of the picture was the caption for the second picture: *"The study hall at Dickson Normal College. The classes were called to and from the class rooms with two rows of electric buttons near the edge of the stage. We assembled in this room for morning exercise. A chapter was read by one of the faculty. We all sang a song or two followed by prayer before starting our day's work."*

Much of the same information from the 1905 bulletin was included in the 1908: Our Location, Positions, Course of Study, Care of Girls, Expenses, and Reasons Why You Should Attend Dickson College. There was much persuasive writing used to encourage parents to send their children.

Professor **E. L. Swank** had three years tenure at Dickson College in the Music Department according to the this bulletin. The Elocution Department was headed by **Miss Mary Barrett** who was trained at Vanderbilt. She was beginning her third year.

One of my favorite sections was "Whereabouts, or What Our Pupils are Doing," for in this section was mention of my Grand Uncle **Thomas Hugh Loggins** who was the son of T.B.'s brother, Henry. (Hugh's picture from Gwen's collection.)

"Dickson College Alumni Doing Well-- "Mr. Hugh Loggins, a graduate of both the Literary and commercial depts. of Dickson College is bookkeeper and stenographer for one of the largest lumber companies in Louisiana. He gets a fancy salary.

in Texas; Prof. **J. C. Terrell**, principal in Stigler, I.T.; **Howard Brown**, lawyer in Dickson**; E. D. Turner** (1905), merchant in Casey Springs; Prof. **R. A Rascoe**, principal in Jemison, Ala.; **Albert Paterson** and **J. B. Davis**, real estate in Walter, Okla., **J. F.**

Duncan, Superintendent Weakley County Public Schools; **T. W. Cleek** (1906), teacher in Louisiana; **Alex King**, proprietor and manager general store in Newbern, Dyer County, Tenn.; Ex-Senator **J. C. Hobbs**, lawyer, farmer, manufacturer in Erin, Tennessee; **J. E. Tubb**, Superintendent Humphreys County Schools; **Rev. Riley T. Davis**, pastor of Baptist Church in Texas; **J. F. Peeler**, principle of Dallas Texas High School for twelve years; **Dr. R. F. Terrell**, practicing medicine in Stigler, I. T.; **Ike B. Hunt** of Maury Co., Tenn., bookkeeper for Post Office Department in Washington City., **J. W. Wilbanks**, (Classic Graduate), pastor of Presbyterian Church, U.S. A. in San Marcos, Tex.; **Judge R. E. Maiden**, attorney for Memphis Street Railway Company; **W. R. Boyte** (Commercial Dept.), cashier of Citizens' Bank in Dickson; **W. T. Killebrew** who served as Circuit Court Clerk of Weakley county was now cashier of Bank of Dresden, Tenn.; **John T. Parrish**, planter in West Tennessee with land in Crockett and Dyer County; **Joel R. Shoffner**, lumber business in Paducah, Ky.; **Bruce L. Rice**, member of cotton firm of F. B. Guest & Co., Wall Street, New York; **Edward Lovell** (Bookkeeping and Shorthand-last year), Nashville, Chattanooga and St. Louis Railway at Nashville, Tenn.; U. S. District Attorney **Casey Todd** with offices in Memphis, Tenn.; **W. T. Fielder**, member of present State Legislature from Hickman Co., and former Dickson Co. representative; **James L. Graham**, membership secretary of Y.M.C.A in Los Angeles, California and president of Epworth League for State of California; **F. F. House**, manager of Whiteville Mercantile Co., in Whiteville, Tenn.; **Clarence Johnson** (combined course in Bookkeeping and Shorthand), position for three years with Southern Iron Co., **Senator O. K. Hollady**, State Senator from Cookeville, Tenn.; **Ira Langly**; clerk of Circuit Court of Clay County, Ark.; **R. S. Bowers** of Gibson Co., Tenn., lawyer in Texas; **S. B. Wofford** of Mississippi (went "West"); Elmer J. Lundy of Arkansas, former chief clerk of Bureau of Statistics for the U. S. Department of Agriculture in Washington, D. C, now (1907) lawyer in Mena, Ark; **B. H. Rawls** (Bookkeeping and Banking Courses), cashier at Palmersville Bank, Palmersville, Tenn.; **Ben Dudley**, lawyer in Norman, Okla.; **E. R. Attkinson** (graduate 16 years before 1907), lawyer in Louisville, Ky.; **O. E. Dabbs** of Georgia (Commercial Course), time keeper for Cincinnati, New Orleans and Texas Pacific Railroad at Chattanooga; and Prof. **J. L. Hutcherson**, teacher in Louisiana, and Prof. **T. O. Brown**, principal of the school where J. L. Huterson teaches in Louisiana.

Another section lists a few of the doctors who studied at Dickson Normal College before becoming medical doctors. They were **Dr. J. R. Fowlkes**, Greenfield,

Tenn.; **Dr. D. T. Gould**, Nashville, Tenn.; **Dr. W. W. Slayden**, Waverly, Tenn.; **Dr. W. J. Sugg**, McEwen, Tenn.; **Dr. L. Thomas**, Paducah, Ky.; **Dr. H. B. Spencer**, Indian Territory; **Dr. George N. Springer**, Hohenwald, Tenn.; **Dr. W. E. and Dr. E. W. Clark**, Mississippi; **Dr. B. F. and Dr. Wylie Walker**, Dickson, Tenn.; **Dr. Dan Pruett**, St. Louis, Mo., **Dr. James Pruett**, Hickman Co., Tenn; **Dr. J. Paul Harvill**, Nashville, Tenn.; **Dr. Clarence Rogers,** Memphis, Tenn., and **Dr. Mack Winchester**, Cairo, Ill.

The 27 March 1908 Dickson County Herald gave a glimpse of the social life of T. B. and Beth:

*"Among those who saw Ben Hur last week are Mr. and Mrs. Copeland, **Prof. Loggins and daughter, Miss Beth**, Mrs. A. C. Hughes, Miss Agnes Duke, Mr. and Mrs. Jas. Haggard."*

The same column in the paper announced an upcoming event at Dickson Normal College:

"Lovers of amusement, will enjoy a splendid treat next Friday night, March 20, when Hal Merton, the great magician, ventriloquist, and entertainer, will appear at the College Hall. Mr. Merton is said to be a most delightful entertainer, and that he can do some stunts that are most mystifying. He is unquestionably a clever actor and the Dickson Lyceum managment [sic] are to be congratulated upon securing this excellent attraction. If you wish to while a way an evening in laughter and fun come out. This will be rich. The next attraction will be Herbert A. Sprague, who comes on March 27. Remember these dates."

The 2 April 1908 issue of the Dickson County Herald carried this Dickson College article with many student names:

"The editorial sanctum of The Herald office was charmingly complimented last Monday afternoon by a visit from the following young lady pupils of the Dickson College, chaperoned by Mrs. Alice Hickman, teacher: Lucile Warren, Myrtle Bouldwin, Florence Bates, Ormie Dunbar, Nannie Swift, Lucy Gillum, Irma Taylor, Flossie Wolfe, Mollie Hays, Christel Bone, Lessie Pate, Creola Baird, Eunice Foley, Jennie Bouldwin, Flora E. Corbitt, Lillian Shaw, Hattie Tucker, Beulah Kendall, Melissie Bassham. The editor soundly appreciates this call from so talented array of Southern beauty and trusts that its repetition may not be far in the future."

The 2 April 1908 Dickson County Herald also promoted the next Dickson Lyceum program: *"Herbert A. Sprague comes to Dickson Friday night as the next attraction on the Lyceum Course. Mrs. Sprague is a reader of rare ability and his long experience in this line insures a good entertainment. His impersonation of Rip Van Winkle is exceptionally fine. Mr. Sprague also presents such plays as David Copperfield, the Rivals and Merchant of Venice. Be sure to hear him at the College Hall Friday night. Caveny, the cartoonist, will be the next attraction on April 6."*

DICKSON LYCEUM.

Herbert A. Sprague comes to Dickson Friday night as the next attraction on the Lyceum Course. Mr. Sprague is a reader of rare ability, and his long expeirence in this line insures a good entertainment. His impersonation of Rip Van Winkle is exceptionally fine. Mr. Sprague also presents such plays as David Copperfield, the Rivals and Merchant of Venice. Be sure to hear him at the College Hall Friday night. Caveny, the cartoonist, will be the next attraction on April 6.

2 April 1908 Dickson County Herald

The following tidbit was in the May 8, 1908 Issue of the Dickson County Newspaper:

"A quiet wedding which seems more or less tinged with romance occurred Wednesday night at the Tulane Hotel in Nashville when Miss Artie A. Bruce and Dr. W. S. Scott were united in marriage. The ceremony was performed by the Rev. W. B. Taylor, pastor of McKendree Chruch and witnessed only by Dr. W.W. Walker and Prof. T. B. Loggins of Dickson. The party returned to Dickson on the 9:00 train the same evening."

[Down On Piney Excerpts from Early Dickson Newspapers and the Dickson County Herald 1883-1916 edited by Georgia L. Baker, 2004]

May 27, 1908 was most surely a proud moment for T. B. and Addie C. Loggins. On that day, Beth Campbell Loggins, number eleven on the program, graduated from Dickson Normal College. Her future husband, Phinous Tilford Rogers, was listed as number sixteen. Beth wouldn't celebrate her eighteenth birthday for another eighteen days. [The following program for Beth's graduation and photograph of Beth were among the family papers and photographs of Henry Loggins, T. B.'s brother. Photo by Thuss, Nashville]

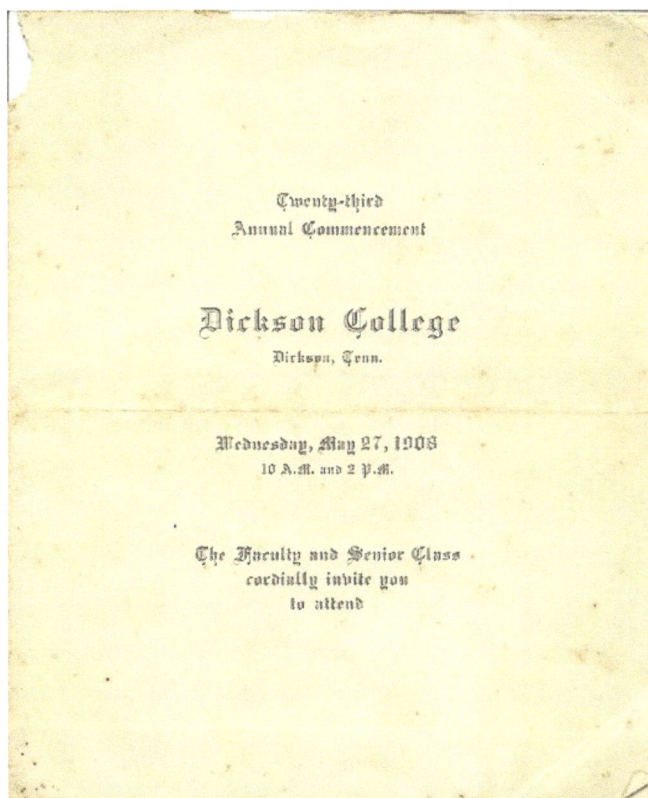

Twenty-third
Annual Commencement

Dickson College
Dickson, Tenn.

Wednesday, May 27, 1908
10 A.M. and 2 P.M.

The Faculty and Senior Class
cordially invite you
to attend

Listed on the inside pages of the program were Hal Bernard, Eunice Lillian Coon, Fred Albert Coon, George Calhoun Collins, Jr., Willie Edna Dickenson, Andy Anderson Eggstein, Tennie May Easley, Franklin Dickson Frazier, Percy Bright Freeman, Webb Goodlen, Beth Campbell Loggins, Doy Bradley Myatt, Porter Edker Odom, Samuel Mathais Rutledge, James Albert Rainbolt, Phineous Tilford Rogers, Walter Marvin Springer, Elmer Claude Stroud, Caleb Harris Sheley, Russell Edwin Wilson, Leon Levelle Wood, Ethel Lettelle wilson, Emma Mabel Williams.

Programme

Music

Invocation

Music

CLASS ORATIONS

1. Hal Bernard . . . . "America's Debt to the World"

2. Eunice Lillian Coon . . . . "From Cave to Palace"

3. Fred Albert Coon . . . . "The Decisive Battle"

4. George Calhoon Collins, Jr. . . . . "The Ethics of a Smile"

5. Willie Edna Dickerson . . . . "Woman's Sphere"

6. Andy Anderson Eggstein . . . . "The Essence of Heroism"

7. Tennie May Easley . . . . "Visions"

8. Franklin Dickson Frazier . . . "Ruskin's Ideas on the Education of Girls"

9. Percy Bright Freeman . . . . . "The Origin of the English Language"

10. Webb Goodlett . . . . "Wit and Humor"

11. Beth Campbell Loggins . . . . "Summer's Heritage"

12. Doy Bradley Myatt . . . . "Longfellow and Evangeline"

13. Porter Edker Odom . . . . "The Veto Power"

14. Samuel Matthias Rutledge . . . "The Power of the Modern Newspaper"

15. James Albert Rainbolt . . . . "China's Awakening"

16. Phinous Tilford Rogers . . . . . "The Future of American Literature"

17. Wauller Marvin Springer . . . . . . "The Twentieth-Century Farmer"

18. Elmer Claude Stroud . . . .
. . . . . "The Future of the Arid Regions of the United States"

19. Caleb Harris Sheley . . . . "Who Ought to be Pensioned"

20. Russell Edwin Wilson . . . . "The Man of Destiny"

21. Leon Levelle Wood . . . . "The Greatest Nation"

22. Ethel Latelle Wilson . . . . "The Power of Music"

23. Emma Mabel Williams . . . . . "How Thor's Hammer Was Broken"

Music

Conferring Degrees

Benediction

The Summer of 1908 was extremely busy for T. B. Loggins. <u>Down On Piney Excerpts from Early Dickson Newspapers and the Dickson County Herald 1883-1916</u> edited by Georgia L. Baker, 2004, page 27 has the following article from the 5 June 1908 Dickson newspaper: *"The Dickson County Institute opened May 28 by Sup. R. E. Corlew at Dickson College with very flattering prospects. Hon. S. E. Hunt was present and addressed the Institute after which work was assigned by the instructors in Charge. For that Institute Prof. T. B. Loggins gave instructions in Grammar, Spelling, Literature, Kern [sic]...Some of the teachers attending were Misses Hattie Cunniff, Clara Donegan, Emma Luther, Junora and Millie Moore, Docke Shipp, Sallie Work; Messrs. Archie Hood, A. F. Patterson, C. J. and M. D. Tidwell and Malcolm Frazier "*

With very little time to rest, T. B. Loggins was in Gibson County, Tennessee to be conductor of the Institute that was held in Milan, Tennessee. Once again he provided a heartfelt report to the State Superintendent. What is also interesting is that in the list of recommendations, T. B. suggested that the State establish Normal Schools that would be under the control of the State Board of Education. When we flash forward to 1912 we will see that his dream becomes a reality when West Tennessee Normal was established.

On the family front, although there is no paper trail, there is no doubt that T. B. visited with his brother, Henry Mitchell, who was living in

Yorkville, Gibson County, Tennessee. Henry's daughter, Mary Loggins who was 23 and living at home, may have even participated in the Institute for she had trained to be a teacher at Dickson Normal School. Clara Brown's 1905 Scrapbook had a picture of Mary Loggins in a group that included Clara Brown.

*" On the college steps. Dickson, Tennessee. Front row left to right **Mary Loggins**, Bert Taylor, Allie Exum, Bertie Pennington. Back row left to right Etta Kilgore, Erma Hays, Lillie May Cavender, Clara Brown, Sydna Bibb Johnson, Cornelia Henning"*

A tidbit in the May 31, 1907 RUTHERFORD REGISTER recorded Mary's participation in a 1907 Teacher Institute: "*Yorkville-Misses Mary Loggins and Annie Pope are in Trenton attending the Teachers Institute.*

The Superintendent's report for the school year ending 30 June 1907 just gave the county: Gibson, dates: May 20-May 30 and the Conductor: J. B. Cummings in a table on page 84.) One of Brother Henry's other big draws was that he had a set of triplets who would turn eight in August. My Grandfather, Reuben Wilson Loggins, was 15. Henry had eight children living at home in 1908. Hugh as already stated was in Louisiana.

BIENNIAL REPORT OF STATE SUPERINTENDANT OF PUBLIC INSTRUCTION FOR TENNESSEE FOR THE SCHOLASTIC YEAR ENDING JUNE 30, 1907-8, pp. 184-187
MILAN STATE INSTITUTE
As conductor of the State Institute held at Milan, June 15 to July 10, 1908, I submit the following report:

There were enrolled in the institute 411 teachers. Of this number Gibson County furnished an even 200. The other 211 came from more than 20 counties in Middle and West Tennessee. The class of teachers seemed better than usual. While there were some too young to teach there was a larger per cent of mature teachers than usual. The scholarship of the body was also and improvement on the institute of the same section a year before. The teachers manifested great zeal and enthusiasm in the work and a desire for better scholarship and more and better professional training was everywhere evident.

Milan is an ideal place for a State Institute. It has ample railroad facilities. The people are as hospitable as ever entertained a body of strangers in their midst. Their homes, which are beautifully and conveniently situated, and the school buildings and accommodations are all that could be desired.

Supt. J. B. Cummings, Supt. C. W. Anderson and Miss Mattie Butler are willing and efficient helpers. Any Conductor of a State Institute who may have their assistance will be fortunate.

The institute thoroughly enjoyed and appreciated the work in agriculture by Prof. Main, of the University of Tennessee. Milan is in a splendid agricultural section, and the work done in this line will bring forth beneficial results.

The institute faculty, the teachers of the institute and the people of Milan were much gratified to have Tennessee's able State Superintendent of Public Instruction present one day, and all were pleased and helped by his splendid and practical address.

Although the institute adopted resolutions on the subject, as Conductor I desire to mention and thank personally, for very valuable assistance, Supt. J. B. Cummings of Gibson County, who induced 200 of his teachers to attend, and who rendered wise counsel in all matters; Supt. E. E. Ellis, of Milan Public School, who was untiring in his efforts and who never lost an opportunity to help; also the splendid entertainment committee, headed by Mr. John Denney and Misses Lena Mills and Wick stone, who met all trains, who secured homes for all and who made the stay in Milan a pleasure. The success of the institute was largely due to their efforts and assistance.

SUGGESTIONS

First--As Conductor I heartily approve the uniform examination for all State Institutes as adopted by the present State Superintendent, and would suggest that if possible such instructions be given conductors and instructors as will bring about, as nearly as possible, uniformity in grading papers and issuing certificates.

Second--Some plan ought to be adopted for those who hold four-year Honor Roll certificates whereby they could take the Reading Circle work yearly without going to State Institutes and yet make their certificates good in all the counties of the State.

Third--That better professional training be furnished the teachers and that a higher grade of qualification be required. This training should be under the control and supervision of the State Superintendent and the State Board of Education. Of course it would be best if the State would make appropriations for this. If not the State Board could establish normal schools, adopt plans, courses, etc., under the present law, and these schools properly managed could be self sustaining. The State now looks largely to self sustaining schools for a supply of teachers. Under the plan here proposed it would be better as the schools could be run under the supervision of the State Superintendent and State Board of Education. T. B. Loggins

FACULTY AND DIVISION OF WORK
       T. B. Loggins, Conductor; Grammar, Physiology, Secondary Literature and Physics.
       J. B. Cummings, Secretary; Arithmetic, U. S. History, Civics and Gilbert's "School."
       W. C. Anderson, Geography, Primary Literature, Rhetoric and Algebra.
       Miss Mattie Butler, Primary Methods.
       Josiah Main, Agriculture.

The 13 November 1908 Dickson County Herald carried the story "Dickson County Teachers Placed."

> *"Following are some of the teachers placed by the Volunteer State Teacher's Agency: Prof. Phinous T. Rogers, who recently graduated from the Dickson College, has accepted a position as a teacher in Central, Ga., near Columbus, where he contemplates teaching for the next six months. This is Mr. Rogers' first school, but we have all reasons to believe that he will succeed to the entire satisfaction of all concerned.* [We can assume that Phinous didn't care much for teaching since it was long before he was enrolled in Pharmacy School.]

Also in the same story was mention of another Dickson Normal School graduate:

> *"Prof. E. N. Harris reports that he is having complete success with his school in the western section of the state. Mr. Harris was for a number of years a student in the Dickson College and has taught for several years in this county."*

T. B.'s brother, Walter Trotter Loggins, also participated in the Teacher Institute that was held in Fayette County,

73

Tennessee from June 22, 1908 to June 27, 1908. The Fayette County report was on pages 242-244: "Prof W. T. Loggins-U. S. History."

The picture on the preceeding page is an old ad for the Dickson Normal College. It was shared on p. 18 of <u>The First Seventy Five A History of the First National Bank of Dickson by</u> Louise Littleton Davis, 1978. Chad Bradford shared a copy of the advertisement to Discovering Dickson County Facebook page on 10 August 2014.

From Davis' book on page 16 we get a glimpse of what the town of Dickson enjoyed because the college was there.

> *"There was a new social life there, with recitals and concerts, plays and lectures for the public on the college campus. Townspeople would dress up for a stroll to the campus for a pleasant evening's entertainment. Or there would be a reception for visiting parents, and open house for all. graduation processions would bring townspeople out to their front porches to watch faculty and graduates file by in their commencement finery."*

According to <u>Patterson's College and School Directory of the United States</u> that was published in 1909 under the heading "Tennessee" on page 320, T. B. Loggins of Dickson, Tennessee was listed as a member of the Tennessee State School Board. R. L. Jones was the Superintendent.

The June 11, 1909 Dickson County Herald printed the story of the Dickson College Commencement on page 1, 4th column right under the paper's name. [The bride in "A Dickson Wedding" was Phineous' sister.]

The Dickson County Herald.

Eight Pages Weekly.   One Dollar a Year.

VOL. 2   DICKSON, TENNESSEE, FRIDAY, JUNE 11, 1909.   NO. 20

National Balloon Race Ends In This County | Charley Wilson Delivers Sermon | Dickson College Annual Commencement | A Dickson Wedding Of Great Interest

The twenty-fourth annual commencement exercises of Dickson College began Sunday morning, May 30, 1909. The baccalaureate sermon was preached by Rev. Reames, now Presiding Elder of the Nashville District, and formerly of this district. The discourse was based upon these words of the Apostle Paul: For I determined not to know any thing among you save Jesus Christ and him crucified." The large audience gave close attention to the sermon so impressive and suggestive. The subject of the evening sermon was "A Scripture Biography." In reviewing the history of Abraham the sterling qualities of true friendship were revealed and dwelt upon at length. The lesson was a most excellent one for young people.

*Regular work was resumed Monday morning. At 8 o'clock in the evening **Prof. and Mrs. Loggins** opened the doors of their lovely home to the students and faculty. In the words of one of the younger boys: "The affair was neither a prayer-meeting nor a courting." and all enjoyed the evening spent in conversation, games, music and readings. At ten o'clock refreshments consisting of ice cream, sherbet and cake were served. At eleven o'clock nearly a hundred joyous, happy students reluctantly bade goodnight to host and hostess and returned to their homes to dream of pleasures passed and to whish might come again.*

Tuesday night the classes in Expression and Music gave their annual recital. The program was interesting and the pupils acquitted themselves with honor.

*Wednesday morning the two graduates, Mr. E. I. Anderson and Miss Carrie Moore, delivered their orations. Mr. Anderson's subject was "A Boy Hero." Miss Moore's "Some Unmarried Women of Note." In the afternoon there was a lawn party which was much enjoyed by the students. At 8:30 in the evening the annual address was delivered by Miss Alice Denslow, of Denver, Tennessee. "The Heritage of the Twentieth Century" was treated in a scholarly, masterful way. After the address Miss Denslow and **Miss Beth Loggins** presented an excellent program. The lovers of the finest of the fine arts were greatly pleased with Miss Beth's selections. **Prof. Loggins** made a few remarks on the school and its future and some plans for its more extensive development.*

*The alumni then elected officers for the approaching year. The following is the list: **Mr. Phinous Rogers, President**; Miss Ida May Reynolds, Vice-President; Mrs. Alice E. Hickman, Secretary; **Mr. T. A. Caraway, Speaker**; Mrs. P. C. Sanders, Alternate Speaker; Dr. Lycurgus Thomas, Toast Master.*

The representatives of the various classes pledged themselves to have their classmates present next June. The Association then adjourned to meet June 1910. A. E. H. [This piece, transcribed from microfilm in the Tennessee State Archives was authored by Alice E. Hickman, secretary of the Alumni Association. Please note also the mention of Thaddeus A. Caraway, future U.S. senator from Arkansas and husband of future Senator Hattie Wyatt Caraway.]

Of the 4 June 1909 Teachers Institute that was held in Dickson, W.A. White, the Dickson County Superintendent, reported on p. 301 of his Report to the Tennessee State Superintendent of Public Instruction that in the

Institute he conducted in Dickson County that T.B. Loggins taught Grammar and Physiology.

The Dickson Normal College reported the following information to the Superintendent of Public Education for Tennessee for the year ending June 30, 1909: *"County: Dickson; Institution: Dickson College, President: T.B. Loggins; Town: Dickson; Teachers: 8; students enrolled: 300; Degrees: B.S., A.B; Age of institution 23 years; Value of property: $10.000; use public funds: no"*

T. B. LOGGINS, A.M., President
Dickson College

In 1909, T. B. Loggins saw that his suggestion in his 1908 Report to the Tennessee State Superintendent *(Third-- That better professional training be furnished the teachers and that a higher grade of qualification be required. This training should be under the control and supervision of the State Superintendent and the State Board of Education.)* became a reality when the General Assembly of Tennessee passed the General Education Bill. The Bill provided funding for establishing public High Schools in each county and for establishing a Normal School in each of the three Grand Divisions of Tennessee. [A copy of the bill may be found in Public School Laws of Tennessee published by Supt. J. W. Brister in 1911. Many of the authors of articles on Dickson Normal College mark this as the "beginning of the end" of D N C, and yes, it was, but, T. B. Loggins championed the cause of public education even though he knew that his own college was probably going to close.

One of my treasured pieces of Great Grand Uncle T.B.'s life is a postcard that my friend Susan Knight Gore found for me from an on-line postcard dealer. It was mailed July 26, 1909 by a student of Dickson Normal College. "The Don't this look natural" comment on the front does show that she may not have listened as well in T. B.'s grammar class as she should have, but the comment does carry a feeling of personal connection. The very picture used to create the postcard was in the photograph collection of my

Great Grandfather, Henry Loggins. That picture is on the Title page of this paper.

The household of T. B. and Addie changed when Beth left for Belmont College in Nashville, Tennessee. She was listed as a member of the "Irregular Class" and the "Tennessee Club" in the 1909 Belmont College Annual.

The latest honor to be conferred on Prof. T. B. Loggins is that which he received Saturday at the hands of Gov. Patterson, who appointed him to succeed P. L. Harned on the State Board of Education. The vacancy was caused by the resignation of Prof. Harned several days ago and honor fell to Prof. Loggins, who is one of the best known educators in the State. Dickson is proud of the recognition Prof. Loggins has received in this instance, and points to the institution of which Prof. Loggins is the principal as being one of the most eulogized and best patronized in the South. Prof. Loggins term will expire March 2, 1913.

"The Topics of the Week" section of the 9 August 1909 issue of the Dickson County Herald. (Copied 28 April 2016 from the Microfilm in the Tennessee State Archives)

The August 9, 1909 Dickson County Herald announced the exciting news that Prof. T. B. Loggins had been appointed to the Tennessee State School board by Governor Patterson.

Prof. W. L. Prince, a well known commercial teacher, will have charge of Bookkeeping, Shorthand and Penmanship at Dickson College. No better advantages can be found anywhere.   20

Miss Alice Denslow, one of the best teachers of Expression in Tennessee, will have charge of the Elocution Department of Dickson College this year. For information, see or write her or T. B. Loggins at Dickson College.

A splendid teacher for the primary grades has been employed at Dickson College for the present year. Your child will be well cared for and well taught. No crowding; splendid equipment. See or write T. B. Loggins for all information.

Dickson County Herald
3 September 1909

The September 3, 1909 Dickson County Herald announced several faculty member appointments for Dickson College: Prof. W. L. Prince, commercial teacher, and Miss Alice Denslow, Elocution teacher.

On October 7, 1909, T. B. Loggins and his wife, Addie C. Loggins, sold to John Galloway and his wife, "*a piece of property near the town of Dickson known as the Mary Murray land in the 5th Civil District of Dickson county, Tenn. bound as follows: Beginning in the line of Patrick Hughes (colored) and running northwardly to the line of Mrs. Mary Cox 96 feet thence westwardly with the line of Mrs. Mary Cox 24 feet thence southwardly with line of Mrs. Cox and others 96 feet to the line of Patrick Hughes and thence Eastwardly with said Hughes line 211 feet to the beginning. Same being a tract of land sold by Patrick Hughes colored and wife Mary Hughes to Mrs. Mary Murray..."* [deed recorded in Register's office at Charlotte Tennessee in Book ?? Pages 6 & 7] The sale of the property was recorded in the Register's Office 8th day of Sept 1921 by T. R. Dickson in Book E, page 84. [Note: The 1910 Census lists this piece of property on Poplar Street. John Galloway's wife was Nettie.]

Another of Dickson Normal School's famous graduates was **Dockie Shipp** who was previously noted as the 1909 Junior Class Secretary. Dockie Shipp, a native of Hickman County, Tennessee, was, according to a Dickson Herald article that was posted to http://www.zoominfo.com/p/Dockie-Shipp/705524026, licensed to teach in Dickson County by the age of eleven. and by age fourteen, she was licensed to teach in the state of Tennessee. [Note: She would have attended State Institutes to achieve the license for Tennessee.] She graduated from Dickson Normal College at the age of sixteen with a B. S. degree. She went on to study Oratory at Vanderbilt and graduated at age eighteen. She spent time on Chautauqua and Lyceum work before returning to the classroom. She worked at Dickson Normal College probably after T. B. Loggins left and then later went on to teach at Dickson High School that was housed in the former Dickson Normal College building. One of Dockie's most famous pupils was her nephew, Frank G. Clement, who served as the Governor of Tennessee. On the second page of four page pamphlet titled "Dockie Anne Shipp ", Dean T. B. Loggins was quoted: *T. B. LOGGINS, M. A., Dean of West Tennessee State Normal, Memphis, Tenn.: I have frequently heard Miss Dockie Anne Shipp read. She has been well trained, is a charming reader, and will delight an audience."*
[http://digital.lib.uiowa.edu/cdm/ref/collection/tc/id/19293]

Laura Wills read old copies Dickson County Herald Newspaper and published eight volumes of abstracts from that paper: <u>Dickson County, Tenn Newspaper Abstracts by Laura Wills</u>. Her publications have been invaluable in researching the lives of T. B., Addie, and Beth during the time from March 1910 until June 1912. The Eight volumes are in the genealogy room of the Dickson County Public Library in Dickson, Tennessee.

> 4 March 1910 Issue-*"Walter Loggins, editor of the Somerville Falcon, spent Monday night here with his brother, Prof. T. B. Loggins and family."* (Laura Wills, Vol. 1, p. 37)
> 25 March 1910 Issue-*"Rev. and Mrs. T. J. Baker entertained Prof. and Mrs. T. B. Loggins and daughter, Miss Beth, accompanied by a*

*number of little folks, at dinner last Sunday, in celebration of the fourth birthday anniversary of their son, Robert Black. The occasion was greatly enjoyed and the young scion of the ministry was a greatly admired personage. (*Laura Wills, Vol. 1, p. 52.
15 April 1910 Issue-*"Delightful Entertainment-Miss Floy Hopkins and Mr. George Collins delightfully entertained a number of their intimate friends last Friday night at the home of the former, to celebrate Miss Hopkins' eighteenth birthday and Mr. Collins' nineteenth birthday. Miss Hopkins was assisted in receiving by Miss Glenn Leech. In the dining room, Miss Glen Hopkins, served fruit punch. Those present were Misses Lucy Wynns, Lucile Ridings, Dee Wilson, Beth Loggins, Edith Badge, Audry Harrison, Oudia Smith, Clayton Smith, Glenn Leech, and Floy Hopkins. Messrs. Lester Rogers, George McMurry, Wade Liggett, Will Meadow, Harry Wynns, and George Collins.* [Laura Wills, Vol. 1, p. 65]

[Note: Floy Hopkins's mother was Fanny Hooper. Fannie's sister was Jessie Hooper. Jessie married Dr. Claude Sizemore. [Clement, p. 51-Claude co-owned Clemmore Pharmacy in Dickson, TN] Claude's mother was Sally Nesbitt Sizemore who served as a Confederate nurse with her husband Rufus Sizemore. Sally's moving letter of serving during the war was included in her Confederate Widow's Pension application. Sally Sizemore was also one of the charter members of the Dickson Cumberland Presbyterian Church. When Floy Hopkins Bouldin was an adult, she wrote a tribute to Sally Sizemore in the Confederate Veteran.]

(1905-Clara Brown Album-no caption)

The 15 April 1910 Federal Census for Dickson, Tennessee (edited) listed the following people as family 17/18 on College Street: Thomas B. Loggins as the head of the family and professor College, Ada C. [sic] as wife, Beth C. as daughter, Josie Hull (age 32, Black) as Private family servant; Mary E. Donegan (age 47, White), housekeeper for College Hill; Maud Outlaw, (age 20, White) waiter for College Dining Hall; Maude Cathey (age 20, Black), Dishwasher for College Dining Hall; Maggie Hannah (age 30, Black), Cook for College Dining Hall. (I included more of the census to show Floy Hopkins, Claud Sizemore, and Rev. T. J. Baker.)

			Name	Relation		Sex	Color	Age	Marital				Language	Occupation	Industry	
	12	13	Baker Thomas J.	Head		m	w	40	m1 13				English	Minister	Methodist church	w
			—— Mary Wm.	wife		F	w	33	m1 13	3	3		English	none		
			—— Thomas B.	Son		m	w	12	S				English	none		
			—— Mary M.	Daughter		F	w	9	S					none		
			—— Robert B.	Son		m	w	4	S					none		
	13	14	Fentress Cecil D.	Head		m	w	32	m1 13				English	Agent	Insurance Co.	w
			—— Ada L.	wife		F	w	31	m1 13	1	1		English	none		
			—— Alline C.	Daughter		F	w	8	S					none		
	14	15	Hooper Melvil W.	Head		m	w	66	m1 40				English	none		
			—— Alice	wife		F	w	57	m1 40	4	4		English	none		
			Sizemore Claude H.	Son in law		m	w	38	m1 12				English	Overseer	Transportation Dept.	w
			—— Jessie A.	Daughter		F	w	33	m1 12	1	1		English	none		
			—— Hooper A.	Grandson		m	w	9	S					none		
			—— Sarah A.	Boarder		F	w	76	wd	3	2		English	none		
	15	16	Hopkins Fannie	Head		F	w	38	wd	4	4		English	Own income		
			—— Floy W	Daughter		F	w	18	S				English	none		
			—— Illen A.	Daughter		F	w	13	S				English	none		
			—— Wren L.	Daughter		F	w	11	S					none		
			—— Ray M.	Son		m	w	7	S					none		
	16	17	Leonard Will. H.	Head		m	w	49	m1 18				English	Sawing	Stave Factory	w
			—— Callie	wife		F	w	39	m1 18	4	4		English	none		
			—— Lucille	Daughter		F	w	10	S				English	none		
			—— Luther	Son		m	w	7	S					none		
			—— Percy	Son		m	w	4	S					none		
			—— Wilber	Son		m	w	½	S					none		
	17	18	Loggins Thomas B.	Head		m	w	47	m1 20				English	Professor	College	Emp
			—— Ada C.	wife		F	w	45	m1 20	1	1		English	none		
			—— Beth C.	Daughter		F	w	19	S				English	none		
			Hull Josie	Servant		F	B	32	m1 4	0	0		English	Servant	Private Family	w
			Donegan Mary E.	Housekeeper		F	w	47	S				English	Housekeeper	College Hall	w
			Outlaw Maude	Servant		F	w	20	S				English	waiter	College Dining Hall	w
			Cathey Maude	Servant		F	B	20	S				English	Dishwasher	College Dining Hall	w
			Hannah Maggie	Servant		F	B	30	S				English	Cook	College Dining Hall	w

Volume 2 of Laura Wills <u>Dickson County, Tenn. Abstracts</u> on page 37 of the abstract for the 27 May 1910 issue: *"Miss Emma Williams of Yellow Creek, is the guest of Miss Beth Loggins"* Emma Williams had served on the Executive Committee for the Class of 1908 with Beth. On page 51, from the summer of 1910 it was reported in Town Tales: *"Mrs. T. B. Loggins and daughter, Beth, are at Dawson's Springs, Ky."* In the 30 June 1910 Issue on page 63 of Vol. 2 was reported *"The following Dickson people attended the Epworth League Convention at Bon Aqua, Monday: Misses Beth Loggins and Dee Wilson."* [notes: The Epworth League was a Methodist young adult association for individuals ages 18–35. Bon Aqua was a popular resort in Hickman County, Tennessee. Dee Wilson was being reared by John Mitchell and Martha Louise Moore Trotter. John Mitchell Trotter was T. B. Loggin's maternal uncle.]

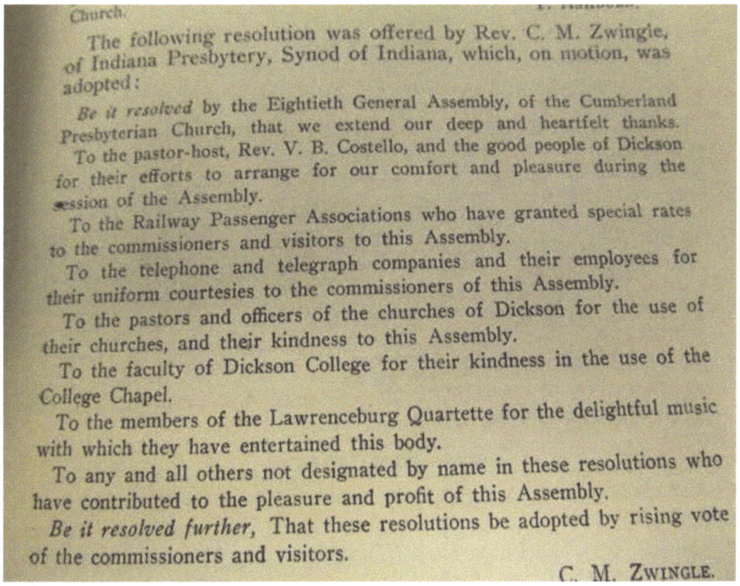
Church.

The following resolution was offered by Rev. C. M. Zwingle, of Indiana Presbytery, Synod of Indiana, which, on motion, was adopted:

Be it resolved by the Eightieth General Assembly, of the Cumberland Presbyterian Church, that we extend our deep and heartfelt thanks.

To the pastor-host, Rev. V. B. Costello, and the good people of Dickson for their efforts to arrange for our comfort and pleasure during the session of the Assembly.

To the Railway Passenger Associations who have granted special rates to the commissioners and visitors to this Assembly.

To the telephone and telegraph companies and their employees for their uniform courtesies to the commissioners of this Assembly.

To the pastors and officers of the churches of Dickson for the use of their churches, and their kindness to this Assembly.

To the faculty of Dickson College for their kindness in the use of the College Chapel.

To the members of the Lawrenceburg Quartette for the delightful music with which they have entertained this body.

To any and all others not designated by name in these resolutions who have contributed to the pleasure and profit of this Assembly.

Be it resolved further, That these resolutions be adopted by rising vote of the commissioners and visitors.

C. M. ZWINGLE.

During the week of May 19-24, 1910, the Eightieth Meeting of the General Assembly of the Cumberland Presbyterian Church set up their tents in Dickson to celebrate the 100th Anniversary of the founding of the Cumberland Presbyterian Denomination in Dickson County, Tennessee on February 4, 1810. One of the tent meetings was rained out so the assembly met in the Chapel of the College.

[In June of 2010 the 180th Meeting of the General Assembly of the Cumberland Presbyterian Church met at Dickson Junior High that had been built on the property of Dickson Normal College. I attended the historic 200th Anniversary of the founding of the Cumberland Presbyterian Church as the President of the Board of the Historical Foundation of the Cumberland Presbyterian and Cumberland Presbyterian Church in America. I had no idea at that time that I was on the campus of the school my Grandfather Loggins had referred to as Uncle T. B.'s school.]

The page pictured is page 59 of the Official Minutes of the 80th General Assembly. These records are housed in the Archives of the Cumberland Presbyterian Church in Cordova, Tennessee.

Volume 3 of Laura Wills Dickson County, Tenn. Abstracts includes several articles: On page 13- 12 August 1910 Issue *"Prof. Loggins and Mrs. T. B. Loggins are spending a vacation at Dawson Springs."* On page 21-26 August 1910 Issue reported in Town Tales *"Miss Beth Loggins is reported quite sick."*[She had Typhoid Fever.] On Page 31-14 October 1910 Issue *"Messrs. W. R. Boyte, James B. Robinson, T. B. Loggins, J. M. Gossett, and Mr. and Mrs. J. A. Clement left Thursday for Clarksville to attend the Methodist Conferences."* On page 39-November 11, 1910 Issue *"Mrs. T. B. Loggins spent Monday in Nashville with her daughter, Miss Beth, who is in Belmont College."* On page 50-December 2, 1910 Issue "*Phinous Rogers attended an entertainment at Belmont College, Nashville Wednesday Night, as a guest of Miss Beth Loggins."*

[This undated picture of Beth with hair decoration was sent to R.B. and Zula Loggins. The picture is now in possession of their descendants in West Columbia, Texas.]

About two years ago, while researching T. B. Addie and Beth, I came across a three-page letter with the envelope that Addie had written on 4 January 1911 on Dickson College stationery for sale on the internet. When I received the letter I was delighted to find that it included so much information about the family as well as giving a glimpse of Great Grand Aunt Addie's delightful personality.

After a bit of research, I was able to locate some information about the recipient of the letter: Mrs. John Brown was Elizabeth Butler Brown. She was born in Tennessee in 1875 and she had married Mr. John B. Brown 10 December 1895 in Sumner County, Tennessee. Rev. R.S. Burwell of the Presbyterian Church performed the ceremony. Stella, who was about 26 at this writing, was Elizabeth's step daughter who married J.E. Hite 15 Nov 1911. Daughter Elizabeth, who was about 10 at this writing, would marry Harry Jackson Renn 4 July 1921 in Sumner County. The Rev. W.C. Cherry performed the ceremony.

My dear Friend-
You sweet little woman, to think of me and take time to do   dainty stitches for me at such a busy time. I certainly do appreciate it and if you knew the glow and warmth that it brought to my heart when I opened the package and read your card and saw what you had done, you would be glad that you kept me in your loving remembrance. The holidays gave me such a heavy heart after the stress of school life, the Fall, and the separation from Beth. I had looked forward to vacation and her return with so much pleasure. Sat. we spent getting the church and tree ready for the children that night. Sunday we did our regular

S. S. and church duties and planning for our Christmas dinner on Monday. Sunday night Mr. L was taken violently ill and after trying all the simple remedies we had to call the Dr. It proved more serious than we at first thought and he was very sick all the rest of the week with gall stones, jaundice and a collapse of the digestive organs. His stomach was so weak that a drink of water would give him pain and a few spoons of soup would cause him to suffer for several hours. He is much better now, and is beginning to eat again. He said he knew an old negro who prayed for it to rain on Sat. night so "niggers" and po white trash wouldn't have to lose no time from the week" We guess This sickness came with the same economical intent during our holidays.

Beth got plump and well after her typhoid, but before she came home had lost her flesh and gone back to the old rut. She has had a rise of temperature every day or so since she came home and has now been in bed three days. She seems some brighter this morning, but still has fever. I feel like I have reached the "end of my ribbon," and don't know what to do with her. School reopens at Belmont today and here she is not able to sit up but a few hours at a time.

Our school opened yesterday and I am perched up on the stage as I write with the rod of authority in my hand and pen in the other. If I should make a mistake and write one of the youngsters a love note and whack you over the head it would be cute wouldn't it? Did Stella come home for Christmas? I guess not, at the distance though I know you enjoyed Elizabeth's vacation and made her enjoy it. You sure enough made my mouth water when you told me about all that good sausage, ribs, bones, etc. My, but how I would like to visit you! Give my best regards to Mr. Brown. Tell Elizabeth the best I can wish for her is to grow to be a woman just like her mother.

Lovingly, Addie C. Loggins

The above picture was cropped from the study hall picture in Clara Brown's 1905 Scrapbook. Addie mentioned in her letter that she was sitting on the stage monitoring Study Hall. I do not know if Addie was included in this 1905 picture.

Dickson College

T. B. LOGGINS, A.M., PRESIDENT

ONE OF OUR SEVEN BUILDINGS

DICKSON, TENN. Jan 4, 1911

My dear Friend,-

You sweet little woman, to think of me and take time to do dainty stitches for me at such a busy time. I certainly do appreciate it and if you knew the glow and warmth that it brought to my heart when I opened the package and read your card and saw what you had done, you would be glad that you that you kept me in your loving remembrance. The holidays gave me such a heavy heart after the strenuous school life of the fall, and the separation from Beth. I had looked forward to vacation and her return with so much pleasure. Sat. we spent getting the church and tree ready for the children that night. Sunday we did our regular S.S. and church duties, and planning for our Christmas dinner on Monday. Sunda

Dickson College

T. B. LOGGINS, A.M., PRESIDENT

DICKSON, TENN.

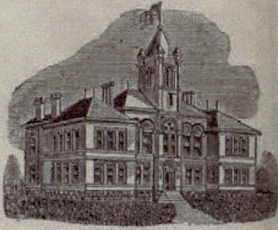

ONE OF OUR SEVEN BUILDINGS

night Mr. L was taken violently ill and after trying all the simple remedies we had to call the Dr. It proved more serious than we at first thought, and he was very sick all the rest of the week with gall stones, jaundice and a collapse of the digestive organs. His stomach was so weak that a drink of water would give him pain, and a few spoons of soup would cause him to suffer for several hours. He is much better now, and is beginning to eat again. He said he knew an old negro who prayed for it to rain on Sat. night so "niggers and po white trash wouldn't have to lose no time from week." We guess his sickness came with the same economical intent, during our holidays.

Beth got plump and well after her typhoid, but before she came home had lost her flesh and gone back to the old rut. She has had a rise of temperature

85

every day or so since she came home and has now been in bed three days. She seems some brighter this morning, but still has fever. I feel like I have reached the "end of my ribbin" and don't know what to do with her. School reopens at Belmont today and here she is not able to sit up but a few hours at a time.

Our school opened yesterday and I am perched up on the stage as I write, with the rod of authority in one hand and pen in the other. If I should make a mistake and write one of the youngsters a love note and whack you over the head, it would be cute, wouldn't it? Did Stella come home for Christmas? I guess not, at the distance, though I know you enjoyed Elizabeth's vacation and made her enjoy it.   You sure enough made my mouth water when you told me about all that good sausage, ribs, bones, etc. My, but how I would like to visit you!

      Give my best regards to Mr. Brown. Tell Elizabeth the best I can wish for her is to grow to be a woman just like her mother.

      Lovingly, Addie C. Loggins.

Reported in the 6 January 1911 Dickson Newspaper (Laura Wills, Vol. 3, page 70) was the marriage of Dee Wilson to Horace H. Self. As stated earlier, Alice Dee Wilson was reared in the household of John Mitchell Trotter, T. B. Loggins' maternal uncle. Dee was the orphaned niece of John Mitchell Trotter's wife, Martha Louisa Moore. J. M. Trotter, who was listed on the Board of Directors of the Waverly Bank and Trust Company of Humphreys County in 12 June 1890 Waverly Times Journal Newspaper, moved to Dickson County by the 1910 Census. He lived on Rickert Avenue which dead ends into College Hill. He and Lou had one daughter, Lellie G. Trotter who had been born in Hustburg, Tennessee in

1869. John Mitchell Trotter served as the administrator of his father's will in March of 1891. Lellie married Walter Ellsworth Miller in Humphreys County 23 December 1891. W. E. Miller was also a prominent educator in the State of Tennessee where he served as President of the McAdow Seminary in Waverly during the 1890's, principal of Fountain City Schools, Superintendent of the Knoxville, Tennessee Schools and Principal of the Snowden School in Memphis, Tennessee. [Picture of Lellie Trotter from collection of R.B. and Zula Loggins, West Columbia, TX-photographer Staples & Co., Church St. Nashville-"Enamel Finish"]

T.B. Loggins must have been very close to John Mitchell and Lou Moore Trotter for in 1904, Lou named T. B. as the executor of his will. She named

R. B. Loggins to serve as executor if for some reason T. B. couldn't. Here are two of the paragraphs from Mrs. J. M. Trotter's will:

October 27, 1904 Mrs. M. Lou Trotter (Probated 13 August 1931)
Fourth, should my daughter, Lellie Trotter Miller died without issue surviving her, then I will and bequeath my said farm and home place above mentioned and all other real estate of which I may die possessed, share and share alike, to Alice Dee Wilson, the daughter of my sister, Moore Wilson, deceased, and to Reubin B. Loggins of Columbia, Texas, and to T. B. Loggins of Dickson, Tenn., sons of my husband's sister, Mary Trotter Loggins, deceased, to have and to hold in fee simple. "

Lastly, I do hereby nominate and appoint T. B. Loggins my executor, and direct that he be exempt from giving bond as such executor. Should the said T. B. Loggins die before this my last will and testament is fully executed, I hereby appoint Reubin B. Loggins as his successor, without bond, and with all powers granted to the said T. B. Loggins. "

Volume 4 of Laura Wills' Transcripts had three separate articles about Beth's very active social life: page 51-10 March 1911 *"Miss Beth Loggins has returned home, after spending several days in Somerville, the guest of her uncle, W. T. Loggins, and family."* page 63-24 March 1911 *"Town Tales: Mr. and Mrs. H. H. Self entertained a number of friends in their new home, Wednesday evening in honor of Miss Virginia Maddox, who is visiting Miss Beth Loggins."* page 64-24 March 1911 *"Albert Talley, the popular express agent at this place, entertained the following young people at supper Sunday evening at the Mays Hotel: Misses Lelia Rogers, Virginia Maddox, of Summerville* [sic: Somerville-Virginia was 18 and the daughter of Edgar A. Maddox, the cashier at the Bank in Somerville.], *Mr. and Mrs. H. H. Self, Messers. P. T. and Lester Rogers.*

Volume 5 of Laura Wills' Transcripts contains the following tidbits: page 50-30 June 1911 *"P. T. Rogers, who has been attending the pharmaceutical department of Vanderbilt University, Nashville, for the past two years, received his diploma last Wednesday. On arrival home that evening he was met at the train by Misses Beth Loggins, Lelia Rogers, Mr. and Mrs. Horace Self and Albert Talley and they went to the John R. Baker spring, south of town where an elegant luncheon was served. Phinous graduated with high honors and his many friends predict for him a successful business career."* Page 58-21 July 1911-*"Miss Beth Loggins entertained for Mr. George C. Collins, Jr., Tuesday evening. The entire affair being carried out in Mr. Collins profession, furniture dealer and undertaker.* Page 65- 21 July 1911 *"Prof. and Mrs. T. B. Loggins and daughter, Miss Beth, left Wednesday for Red Boiling Springs.*[A resort town in Macon County, Tennessee.]

BULLETIN OF

DICKSON COLLEGE

Devoted to the Interests of the Patrons and Pupils of Dickson College and the Cause of Education Generally   DICKSON, TENN.   WISDOM IS MORE PRECIOUS THAN GOLD

T. B. LOGGINS, A.M.
President, Dickson College

W. J. DAVIES, A.B.
History, Mathematics, Greek, Dickson College

Postcard courtesy of the Ragan Family Historical Photograph Collection.

The final <u>Bulletin of Dickson College</u> was published some time in the summer of 1911 for it advertized the Twenty-Seventh Year was to begin on Thursday, August 31, 1911. The Bulletin still had the picture of the main building on the front page but the pictures of President T. B. Loggins and Prof. W. J. Davies, A. B. were at the top of the first Page. The course outline for both the Teacher courses, degree courses and Commercial Courses were much the same but the teachers for each subject were given in "The Course in Detail" section. Prof. W. J. Davies, A. B. taught Mathematics, Mrs. Alice E. Hickman, A. B. taught History (United States, Tennessee, English, French , and Ancient, Miss Alice Davies taught "Department of Expression and Physical Culture; and Prof. D. L. Swank continued to be the head of the Music Department. T. B. Loggins shared English teaching duties with Mrs. Alice E. Hickman, A. B. Every piece of literature for each of the years was listed in the Bulletin. T. B. Loggins was the sole teacher for the Sciences.

"The Sciences are taught after the most modern methods. The course extends over four years and includes Physiology, Botany, Geology, Physics, and Chemistry. A specialty is made of Physiology, and our pupils learn the subject practically and thoroughly. Manikins, charts, drawings, and dissections are used to aid the work. Botany is taught in the class room and also in the field and woods. Flowers are analyzed, traced, and mounted. Our pupils acquire a working knowledge of Botany that will enable them to study alone the flora of any community. Geology is taught not only in the class room, but also in the fields. The vicinity of Dickson, with its caves and sixty varieties of rocks, minerals, and fossils, furnishes an excellent place for the study of Geology. Physics and Chemistry are taught from the texts and by experiments. Pupils will do a large

amount of laboratory work in these branches. The work in the Sciences in Dickson College is practical and comprehensive."

In the Faculty article, T. B. wrote the following information:

> *"We call special attention to the very strong Faculty chosen for the next school year. All of the teachers are well known, not only to the management, but also throughout the State. Nearly all of them have taught in Dickson College for years.*
> *Prof. W. J. Davies, Mrs. Alice Hickman, and Prof. D. L. Swank, who have been with the school so long and who have rendered such valuable and satisfactory service, and who by their able teaching, sympathetic dealings, exemplary, Christian lives, have helped and blessed so many Dickson College pupils, will remain with the school.*
> *Miss Alice Davies, a well-trained and experienced teacher, will have charge of the class in expression"*

Notes: **Prof. David L. Swank** continued to live in Dickson, Tennessee where he died September 30, 1930. He is buried in the Union Cemetery in Dickson in Plot: Helberg, A-30-3 (Find a Grave Memorial # 126687717.)

William J. Davies and **Alice Davies** were brother and sister. They lived on Rickert St. in 1910. On 28 August 1912 in Obion County, Tennessee, W. J. married **Mrs. Alice Hickman**. Rev. S. F. Wynn performed the ceremony. In 1915 W. J. Davies was listed as the principal of West Tennessee College in Dyer, Gibson County, Tennessee. (Source: page 41, The University of Tennessee Register, published in April 1915.) William J. Davies, born 22 September 1864 in Kentucky, died in Martin, Tennessee on 11 August 1940. His Find A Grave Memorial is # 65986477. He was listed as College teacher on the 1940 Martin, Weakley County Census and his death certificate.

Alice M. Davies, born 11 October 1855 in Kentucky, died in Martin, Weakley County, Tennessee on June 11, 1931. Her brother, William J. Davies, signed as informant. Her Find A Grave Memorial is # 20947772.

Mrs. Alice Hickman, as mentioned above, married Prof. W. J. Davies. They had one daughter, Mary Hamilton Davies. She was born 24 June 1913 in Tennessee. Mary Hamilton Davies was in the 1932 Sophomore Class at University Tennessee at Martin. Her picture is on page 29 in the yearbook. According to the Social Security records, Mary H. died, never having married, in August 1979 in Martin, Weakley County, Tennessee.

In the 1911 paper, there was a section called "Medals." The purpose was "to encourage pupils to a greater effort." Each of the medals was a ten-dollar gold medal. There were ten medals available:

Scholarship Medal provided by President Loggins for the student with the highest average; W. H. McMurray Medal provided by the president of the Citizens' National Bank for pupil with highest average in deportment attendance, and punctuality; S. E. Hunt Medal provided by the cashier of the First National Bank of Dickson for pupil who writes and delivers the best original speech on any theme; U. D. C. Medal provided by the Old Hickory Chapter of Dickson Daughters of the Confederacy for the pupil who will write and deliver the best paper on a theme connected with the South, its people, heroes, or literature; John M. Smith Medal was provided for the pupil in Elocution Class who was the most proficient in Expression; V. B. Miller Medal was for the student who gave the declamation. (debating); W. R. Boyte Medal provided by cashier of Citizens' National Bank of Dickson for making the best declamation; and A. H. Leathers Medal for student who showed the greatest proficiency in piano. In addition the Clemore Pharmacy provided a medal for best piano student. Mr. W. T. Rogers provided a medal for the student who showed the most proficiency with a stringed instrument. [W. T. Rogers was Phineous Tilford

E-Bay listing of an item that sold 16 April 2016 from the personal collection of the person who listed the item, paulj1955. The bottle measures 5 inches long.
Bottle Text: Clemore Pharmacy "The Rexall Store" Dickson, Tenn

Rogers' father. p. 34, Robert S. Clement: W. T. had been elected School Director for city of Dickson May 20, 1901. p 109, Robert S. Clement: Clemore Pharmacy owned by W.A. "Billy" Clement and Claude Sizemore.]

T. B. Loggins provided a list of references: Rev. H. B. Reams, presiding elder of the Nashville District, Nashville, Tenn.; Dr. W. M. Anderson, former pastor of First Presbyterian in Nashville, Tenn.; Elder T. B. Larimore, of the Christian Church in Nashville, Tenn.; Rev. Wh. H. Johnston, Presiding Elder of the Fayetteville District, Fayetteville, Tenn.; Rev. W. B. Taylor, former pastor of McKendree Church in Nashville, Tenn.; **Judge T. H. Caraway, Jonesboro, Ark.;** Judge R. E. maiden, Dresden,

Tenn., Norman M. Byars, attorney, Memphis, Tenn.; Ex-Senator J. C. Hobbs, Erin, Tenn.; **Capt. S. A. Mynders, Ex-Superintendent of Schools of Tennessee, president of West Tennessee Normal School, Memphis, Tenn.;** Dr. Wickliffe Rose, Peabody Board, Washington, D. C.; Prof J. B. Cummings, Superintendent of Gibson Co. Schools, Trenton, Tenn.; Prof. R. E. L. Bynum, Superintendent of Madison County Schools, Jackson, Tenn.; Superintendent J. E. Tubbs, Superintendent of Humphreys County Schools, Waverly, Tenn.; Superintendent Fred J. Page, Superintendent of Williamson County Schools, Franklin, Tenn.' R. S. Bowers, attorney in Caldwell, Texas; Senator O. K. Holladay of Cookeville, Tenn.; Elder J. C. McQuiddy, editor of Gospel Advocate, Nashville, Tenn.; United States Senator R. L. Taylor, Nashville, Tennessee; and Ex-Gov. Benton McMillin, Nashville, Tenn.

There were five photographs in the paper: "A Picnic Party of Teachers and Pupils Under a Cliff of Solid Limestone 200 Feet High," "Botany and Geology Classes on an Excursion on the Creek a Few Miles from Dickson," "Actual Scene in Our Commercial College-Pupils at Work," and "The Crescent and Star Basket-Ball Teams." The final picture was of some of the faculty and fourteen members of the Senior class who graduated in the Literary Department at the close of the school year: May 31, 1911. Prof. Loggins and Mr. Davies are seated in the front. The students who were pictured were Florence Armour, Ella Baker; Malcolm Frazier; Huron Brandon, W. T. Fulton, Ida Hutchison, A. L. Holmes, Amos Johns; Clyde Lunn; Otto Milam; Lucile Ridings; Donald Sensing, Virginia Smith and Lida Rogers. [Lida was the sister of Phineous.]

An interesting fact present in the paper was "*Twenty-two years ago Miss Mary McCrary graduated from this school. This year Donald McCrary Sensing, her son graduated.*"

Prof. Loggins refers to the future West Tennessee State Normal School in the paper "*If you expect to attend the West Tennessee Normal School at Memphis in 1912, you should by all means enter Dickson College on August 31, 1911. No other school can or will connect so well with that school as Dickson College.*" and "*Don't forget that Dickson College is the school for West Tennessee teachers for the school year 1911-1912, if they expect to attend the West Tennessee State Normal School when it opens.*" and "*Do you expect to attend the West Tennessee State Normal School at Memphis when it opens? Then come to Dickson on August 31, 1911, and we will prepare you as no other school can.*"

DICKSON COLLEGE
For Both Sexes

An institution patronized by the best people of the land and indorsed by them. Gives to young men and young women a thorough, practical, economical, sensible education.

The Lowest Rates of Any First-class Institution in the South

In the previous years, Dickson Normal School's student body had been at capacity for the buildings but for the 1911 School Year, T. B. decided to scale back the enrollment. *"After years of experience and much observation, we are convinced that it is best to limit the numbers of the school. We have, therefore, decided to receive only two hundred and fifty pupils in school."*

Several Sections in the Bulletin address behavior of the students and care for the students.

CARE OF THE PUPILS

In the first place, parents desire that their children shall be well cared for. This Dickson College doe. Under our plan and arrangement of our buildings pupils are constantly under the care and guidance of teachers. They are cared for in sickness and in health, and every need supplied."

WORK OF PUPILS-Parents also desire to know that their children will work while in school. This is a feature with Dickson College. Our pupils are required to do their work. They form habits of study and work while here, and also work when they go out into the world. If we cannot get pupils to work, we notify parents and advise them to take their children from school.

DEPARMENT FOR BOYS-We have four commodious and comfortable well-lighted and ventilated dormitories in which most of our boys and young men board. These buildings are situated on the college grounds, and are under the immediate care and control of the President and his assistant teachers both day and night. Boys in these dormitories will be off the streets, will have study hours, and will be required to conform to a high degree of discipline. Teachers will room in these buildings and will assist the President in seeing that every boy is in his place and does his work and conforms to the requirements of study and rest every hour of the day and night. After an experience of twenty-five years, the President feels that he knows what is best; and while he will allow some boys to board in town, yet he urges parents to place their sons on the college grounds, knowing that they will do better work, be under better discipline, and be better cared for in sickness, and rally be happier and accomplish more in their studies."

93

T.B. outlined for whom Dickson College was designed by addressing how DNC prepared future lawyers, physicians, business man, and teachers. T. B. also realized that many young people were undecided. Of them he said,

> *"Dickson College is a school for the masses. To those who wish to enter a special line of work it gives first a thorough general preparation-a complete literary course-and then directs them in the line of their specialties. Many people, however, are in school and many more will go to school who have not decided what they will do in life....Some people need a complete college course to help them to choose."*

T. B. also realized that the agrarian society was changing when he included this section:

"The Future Farmer."

"The time has come when the farmer, too, needs training. Agriculture has made more rapid strides of late years than any other calling. Time was when the man who could plow and hoe was a farmer, but not so now. No class of people in the world need a broader education than the farmer. He must know how to think; he must know how to express himself; he must know his soil, its chemical analysis, he must know his fertilizers and their analysis; he must know his crops; he must know the best breeds of animals and how to feed and care for them; he must be an executive; he must be the broadest-minded man in the community. The farmer is needed, too, by the public. NO better life in our American nation can be found than that found on the farms. The farmers are needed in our legislature, they are needed in Congress, they are needed as Governors and as United States Senators. The farmer needs the training; the world needs the farmer. Dickson College especially invites the farmer and the farmer's boy to seek its advantages.

[T.B.'s progressive thinking absolutely amazes me in the above section about The Future Farmer. What he said in 1911 is very true of today's 2016 Farmer. His brothers, Will, Henry, W.T. and Reuben still either made their living or dabbled in farming in 1911.]

T.B. was very concerned about the safety of his female students. Clara Brown in her 1905 scrapbook included a picture of girls on an outing. Her comments on the picture illustrated the following paragraph that was in the Bulletin of Dickson Normal School.

DEPARTMENT FOR GIRLS-

No better arrangements for the education of girls and young women can be found than at Dickson College. They have a separate building in which only they and lady or married teachers reside. The rooms are neatly furnished, well lighted and ventilated. The girls and young ladies of the

94

school never leave the campus, except in company with a teacher; never visit in the town, never receive company from young men unless the parents request it in writing; and even then the President, being on the ground and knowing the conditions, reserves the right to prohibit it if, in his judgment, it is best for the girl in question or for the school. Girls of Dickson College are carefully managed as it is possible."

Sunday afternoon while out for a walk Feb. 1906 The man is one of the teachers Pro. Perdue. The girls were not allowed to go for a walk with out one of the teachers

Pictured left to right: Camille Henning (Jackson, Tenn.), Clara Brown (Union City, Tenn.), Sallie Spencer (Athens, Georgia), Allie Exum (Jackson, Tenn.), Leona Arnold (Jonesboro, Arkansas),Mr. R. E. Purdue (Franklin, Kentucky), Etta Gilgore (Martin, Tenn.), Lillie Mae Cawnder (Dukedom, Tenn.) Connee Pitty (Kennett, Missouri), Lillian Clinard (Greenbrier, Tenn.), Bertie Remington (Ripley, Tenn.)

I have chosen to include this copy of the copy of the picture from the 1911 Bulletin because T.B. Loggins was shown on the first row, third man from the left. Prof. Davies was the second man from the left. I would hazard to guess that Prof. Swank was the man to T. B.'s right. T. B. stated that there were 14 (six girls and eight boys) students in the photograph. The other seven were faculty but no faculty names were given.

On page 79 of the <u>Milady in Brown</u>, 1910-1911, Beth Loggins was pictured as a member of the Tau Phi Sigma Sorority. She was also listed on 163 as a member of the S.C.S. R. R. organization. Beth's picture is on the second row, the first girl on the left. [note: The only jewelry she wore at her wedding was her sorority pin.]

96

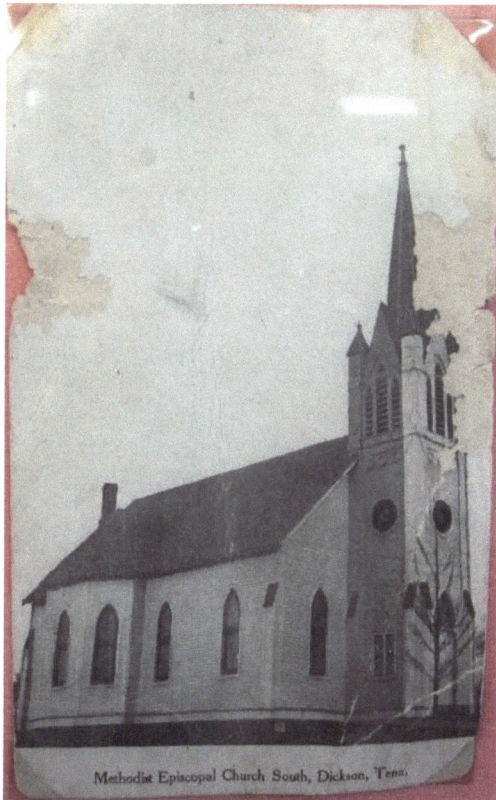
Methodist Episcopal Church South, Dickson, Tenn.

"Mrs. Blanche Petty and Mrs. T. B. Loggins attended Quarterly Conference of the Methodist Episcopal, South at Fagen's Chapel Monday." [Laura Wills, Vol. 6, p. 11]Addie was quite active in the Methodist Episcopal, South, In the Second Annual Report of the Woman's Missionary Council of the Methodist Episcopal Church, South, for 1911-1912 on pages 456-457, Mrs. T. B. Loggins, Dickson, Tenn. was listed as the Corresponding Secretary, Foreign Department for the Methodist Episcopal Woman's Missionary Council. From early Dickson County Abstracts already cited and Addie's letter, it is obvious that the three family members participated in the activities of the Methodist Episcopal, South in Dickson. (Postcard courtesy of the Ragan Family Historical Photograph Collection) Another source for Addie's Church Work follows: *Methodist Episcopal WOMAN'S MISSIONARY COUNCIL. Corresponding Secretary, Foreign Department, Mrs. T. B. Loggins, Dickson, Tenn.* [pp. 456-7. Second Annual Report of the Woman's Missionary Council of the Methodist Episcopal Church, South, for 1911-1912]

Beth had quite an active social life during the late summer and early fall of 1911. Volume Six and Seven of Laura Will's Dickson County Abstracts have numerous articles.

p. 17-18: 25 August 1911 Issue-*"An outing was given at Ruskin Thursday in honor of Misses Maude Kindle and Alberta Cooper, of Nashville, who are the quests of Miss Beth Loggins. Those enjoying the day were: Misses Albert Cooper, Maude Kindle, Beth Loggins, Lyda Rogers, Lelia Rogers, Ouida Smith, Vallie Henslee, Edith Badge; Messrs. George Collins, Lester Rogers, Will Meadow, Dr. Weaver, Max Ramsey of St. Louis, and H. T. Cowan."*

p. 20: 1 September 1911 Issue-*"Miss Lelia Rogers, entertained, Friday evening, in honor of Beth Loggins' charming visitors, Misses Alberta Cooper and Maude Kindle of Nashville. Progressive Rook was the feature of the evening. Miss Beth Loggins winning the prize, which was one of *McCutcheon's books, The Butterfly Man. Those present were: Mr. and Mrs. Raymond Joslin; Misses Glenn Leech,*

Beth Loggins, Alberta Cooper, Maud Kendal, Clayton Smith, Vallie Henslee, Lyda Rogers, Ouida Smith, Edith Badge; Messrs. Turner Cowan, Max Ramsey of St. Louis; Lester Rogers, Walter Rogers, George Collins, William Meadow, Edward Henslee."

[*The fictional work, <u>The Butterfly Man,</u> by George Barr McCutcheon was a published in 1910.]

p. 21: 1 September 1911 Issue-*"The following young people enjoyed Sunday at Bon Aqua: Misses Lelia Rogers, Alberta Cooper, BethLoggins, Maud Kindle, Messrs. Lester Rogers, C. S. Key, D. D. Dunn and George Collins, Jr."*

p. 47: 3 November 1911 Issue-*"The Embroidery Circle gave a Hallowe'en Party at the beautiful residence of Mr. and Mrs. H. H. Self on West College Street Tuesday Night. The guests, masked as ghosts, were received by a ghost who served frappe, after which the witches conducted them to a gypsy tent where fortunes were told. After unmasking, an elaborate two course menu was served. The table was decorated with fruit, pumpkins and black cats. Then before the fire, chestnuts were roasted and ghost stories were told. Those present were Misses Beth Loggins, Ouida Smith, Suzanne McCaul, Glenn Katie Clay Crow, Clayton Smith, Vallie Henslee, Edith Badge, Lucy Hold, Gertrude and Mabel Self and Hattie Ridings. Messrs. Turner Cowan, William Meadow, Hugh Wynns, J. A. Pope, Albert Talley, G. L. Bouldin, Clyde Self, Lester Rogers, Harry Wynns, George Donegan, George Collins, Cecil Self."*

p. 56: 17 November 1911 Issue-*"Mrs. Pitt Henslee, assisted by Miss Vallie Henslee, entertained Friday morning with a luncheon in honor of Misses Birdie Lee Roberts and Katie Clay Crow from Pulaski, the guests of Miss Floy Hopkins. Progressive hearts was played, the scores being kept in a novel fashion, by dropping tiny pieces of candy into bottles. Those present were Misses Lelia and Lida Rogers, Beth Loggins, Ouida Smith, Floy Hopkins, Clayton Smith."*

p. 71: 8 December 1911 Issue-*"Miss Anne Forbes, after a several days' visit here with Miss Beth Loggins, has returned to her home in Hopkinsville, Ky. She was accompanied home by Miss Beth, who will be her guest several more days."*

Vol 7, p. 22: 12 January 1912 Issue-*"Miss Beth Loggins entertained the Sewing Circle with Progressive Rook last Friday evening. Miss Vallie Henslee was awarded a beautiful hand embroidered jabot, having made the highest score. A delightful two course menu was served at the card tables. The members of the Circle present were Misses Susanne McCaul, Ouida Smith, Lelia and Lida Rogers. Visitors were Misses Clayton Smith, Vallie Henslee."*

Beth's Wedding

The Friday, May 24, 1912 Issue of the <u>Dickson Herald</u> carried the following announcement: *"Prof. and Mrs. T. B. Loggins announced the approaching marriage of their daughter, Miss Beth, to Phinous T. Rogers. The marriage is to take place on June 26th at the home of the bride's parents."* [Laura Wills, Vol. 8 Dickson County Abstracts, p. 22]

I didn't have to rely upon Laura Wills for the newspaper article that covered the wedding that she included on page 41 of her Volume 8 of Dickson County Abstracts, for it was in a set of pictures that Alex Leech gave my mother that had been in the home of his Grandfather, Will Loggins, in Tiptonville, Tennessee. The name of the paper was not included with the clipping.

In the story please note the following: Phinous has simplified his name to Finis. Prof. Swank sings. Two of T. B.'s sisters-in-law, Ethel McCauley Loggins, wife of J. T, and Jennie Cocke Loggins, wife of W. T., helped Addie with the wedding. Beth's Matron of Honor was Dee Wilson Self, who was the niece reared by Beth's grand uncle, John Mitchell Trotter. Clyde Davies, who was about eight, was the son of Prof. W. J. Davies. Lelia Rogers, Lyda Rogers and Lester Rogers who are Finis' siblings all participated in the service. Rev. D. E. Hinkle was a minister in the Methodist Episcopal South. Mrs. Finger of Ripley, Mississippi was Bertha Wright Rogers, Finis's sister who married within the same week as Finis and Beth graduated from Dickson College in 1909. Professor Swank has sung for Bertha's wedding and Lelia Rogers had played for the wedding of her sister, Bertha.

"ROGERS-LOGGINS

*At the lovely home of her parents, **Prof. and Mrs. T. B. Loggins**, on College Hill, the marriage of **Miss Beth Campbell Loggins** to **Mr. Finis Tilford Rogers** was solemnized Wednesday evening June 28, at 8:30 o'clock, **Rev. D. E. Hinkle** of Nashville, performing the ceremony.*

*The spacious reception hall was beautifully decorated with maiden hair ferns, field daises and potted plants. The arch from which hung the letters L. and R. was in a mass of sweet peas intertwined with ferns. The hanging gates to the doors added much to decorations and were opened by **Master Clyde Davies** and **Junior Graham** and held open for the bridal* *party. The bride and her party entering the left gate and the groom and groomsman entering the gate at the right crossing in front of the altar formed an isle for the bride and groom.*

*Miss **Lelia Rogers**, sister of groom, wearing a very becoming gown of blue satin presided at the piano in her usual charming manner. **Prof. D. L. Swank** rendered very beautifully "My Rosary" and "I Love You Truly."*

*Miss **Lyda Rogers**, sister of groom, wore a very especially becoming dress of pink crepe de chene over pink satin trimmed with roses and carrying white carnations. She was followed by the maid of Honor, Miss **Alberta Cooper** of Nashville, who wore an elegant green satin with over-dress of white chiffon with gold-dotted designs and pearl trimmings. Her flowers were pink carnations.*

*__Mrs. Horace Self__, Matron of Honor, was handsomely gowned in a white crepe de chene over white satin entrain with bands of point lace trimmings and carried white roses. She was followed by the bride who never looked more beautiful than on this occasion in her exquisite gown of white chamoise satin entrain with trimmings of point lace. Her dainty tulle veil gracefully draped was held in place by a beautiful sunburst given her by her parents. Lilies of the Valley were used with her veil. The brides only ornament was her jeweled sorority pin. The groom, and groomsmen, **Mr. Lester Rogers** and **Mr. Clark Suter**, wore the usual tuxedo suits and entered the door at the right. The attendants formed the aisle thru which the bride and groom wended their way to the arch were the ceremony was performed by Rev. Hinkle in a very impressive manner.*

This happy union was witnessed by a great number of relatives and friends.

*Misses **Christine Hunt** and **Mabel Self** served frappe during the evening. Immediately after the ceremony a reception was tendered them by Mrs. Loggins, mother of the bride, being assisted by **Mrs. J. T. Loggins**, Angleton, Texas, **Mrs. W. T. Loggins**, Somerville and **Mrs. J. L. Graham**.*

*The guests were met at the door by **Mrs. Finger** of Ripley, Miss., **Mrs. Hogins** and **Mrs. McCaul.***

They received very elegant presents of cut glass, brass, silver, china and linen.

Miss Beth is the only daughter of Prof. and Mrs. T. B. Loggins and counts her friends by her acquaintance. This is one of the best known families of Tennessee, Miss Beth is a very strong Christian character and has every charm to make a happy home for the man of her choice. Mr. Rogers is from a very fine family and is a devoted Christian young man of high morals and is indeed to be congratulated upon winning such a prize.

Miss Loggins and Mr. Rogers received part of their education at the Dickson   College, of which her father is President. She afterwards went to Belmont and Mrs. Rogers graduated last year from Vanderbilt University in Pharmacy. He is now located in Chattanooga where they will make their home. May heaven's richest blessing be on this happy couple."

One of the gifts of china that Beth and Finis received was a Chocolate set that Zula Winstead Loggins, T.B.'s sister-in-law, painted. When Beth Loggins Roger's friend, Leta Weaver, was going through Beth's estate, she sent the chocolate set to Zula's granddaughter, who was also a Beth Loggins before marriage. The chocolate set is now with Beth Loggins Roberts. Beth sent me these pictures of this treasured heirloom.

Here are several photos of the chocolate set Zula painted for Beth's wedding in 1912. Tried to take a close-up so you could see the pattern. It is beautiful.

Rogers-Loggins.

At the lovely home of her parents, Prof. and Mrs. T. B. Loggins, on College Hill, the marriage of Miss Beth Campbell Loggins to Mr. Finis Tilford Rogers was solemnized Wednesday evening June 26, at 8:30 o'clock, Rev. D. E. Hinkle of Nashville, performing the ceremony.

The spacious reception hall was beautifully decorated with maiden hair ferns, field daisies and potted plants. The arch from which hung the letters L. and R. was a mass of sweet peas intertwined with ferns. The hanging gates io the doors added much to decorations and were opened by Master Clyde Davies and Junior Graham and held open for the brtdal party. The bride and her party entering the left gate and the groom and groomsmen entering the gate at the right crossing in front of the altar formed an aisle for the bride and groom.

Miss Lelia Rogers, sister of groom, wearing a very becoming gown of blue satin presided at the piano in her usual charming manner. Prof. D. L. Swank rendered very beautifully "My Rosary" and "I Love You Truly."

Miss Lyda Rogers, sister of groom, wore a very especially becoming dress of pink crepe de chene over pink satin trimmed with roses and carrying white carnations. She was followed by the Maid of Honor, Miss Alberta Cooper of Nashville, who wore an elegant green satin with over-dress of white chiffon with gold-dotted designs and pearl trimmings. Her flowers were pink carnations.

Mrs. Horace Self, Matron of Honor was handsomely gowned in a white crepe de chene over white satin entrain with bands of point lace trimmings rnd carried white ioses. She was followed by the bride who never looked more beautiful than on this occasion in her exquisite gown of white chamoise satin entrain with trimmings of point lace. Her dainty tulle veil gracefully draped was held in place by a beautiful sunburst given her by her parents. Lillies of the valley were used with her veil. The brides only ornament was her jeweled sororite pin. The groom, and groomsmen, Mr. Lester Rogers and Mr. Clark Suter, wore the usual tuxedo suits, and entered the door at the right. The attendants formed the aisle thru which the bride and groom wended their way to the arch where the ceremony was performed by Rev. Hinkle in a very impressive manner.

This happy union was witnessed by a great number of relatives and friends.

Misses Christine Hunt and Mabel Self served frappe during the evening. Immediately after the ceremony a reception was tendered them by Mrs. Loggins, mother of the bride, being assisted by Mrs. J. T. Loggins, Angleton, Texas, Mrs. W. T. Loggins Somerville and Mrs. J. L. Graham.

The guests were met at the door by Mrs. Finger of Ripley, Miss., Mrs. Hogins and Mrs. McCaul.

They received very elegant presents of cut glass, brass, silver, china and linen.

Miss Beth is the only daughter of Prof. and Mrs. T. B. Loggins and counts her friends by her acquaintance. This is one of the best known families of Tennessee. Miss Beth is a very strong christian character and has every charm to make a happy home for the man of her choice. Mr. Rogers is from a very fine family and is a devoted christian young man of high morals and is indeed to be congratulated upon winning such a prize

Miss Loggins and Mr. Rogers received part of their education at the Dickson College, of which her father is President. She afterwards went to Belmont and Mr. Rogers graduated last year from Vanderbilt University in Pharmacy. He is now located in Chattanooga where they will make their home. May heavens' riches blessings be on this ha

Beth's and Finis' wedding was also announced on page 168 of the Vanderbilt University Quarterly, Vol. 13. in the "Alumni Notes" section. "(Class of) *1911-The marriage of Miss Beth Campbell Loggins, of Dickson, Tenn., to P. T. Rogers, PhC, took place June26, 1912."*

Beth's wedding announcement stated that she and Finis would be living in Chattanooga. Two sources support that Finis was employed in that city. First, the 1912 Chattanooga Directory of Chattanooga, Tennessee listed *"Rogers, Finis T, clerk St Elmo Drug Co, r. 105 St. Elmo av, St E."* Second, the American Druggist and Pharmaceutical Record, Volume, 60-January to December 1912 included the following announcement on page 86:

> *"The interest of W. F. Wessenberg in St. Elmo Drug Company, of Chattanooga, has been purchased by **Finis T. Rogers** and I. E. Blevins. The business will be under the active charge of Barton Jones, who has been associated with the St. Elmo Drug Company for the past four years."*

****

Planes, Trains, and Automobiles: August 4, 2016, Beth Loggins Roberts brought me the shower gift that her grandmother Zula Winstead Loggins had sent to Beth in 1912 for one of Beth's bridal showers. The bowl rode from Columbia, Texas to Dickson, Tennessee on a train. Beth moved the bowl with her to Chattanooga. She would have then packed the bowl for its move to Memphis, Tennessee. Later the bowl moved with Beth and Phineous to Phoenix, Arizona where it remained until Beth's death. Beth's friend gave the bowl to Beth Loggins Roberts. The older Beth and the younger Beth had become close since they shared a name. Fast forward to 2016 when Beth, the younger, took the bowl to West Columbia, Texas by car so that she could bring the treasured family heirloom to me. Beth and her sister-in-law, Donna, carefully wrapped the bowl so they could carry it on the plane to Memphis, Tennessee.
****

The spring and summer of 1912 had been very busy for the T. B. and family. Not only were they planning a wedding, T. B. began actively working to help set up West Tennessee State Normal School in Memphis, Tennessee. Otis Jones discussed the early school preparations on **Page 82** in 1911-1925 West Tennessee State Normal School.

"On April 25, 1912, Dean Thomas B. Loggins arrived at the school to begin the work of preparing for opening classes, which, no doubt, it was hoped to get underway in the summer of 1912. Professor Loggins had been head of Dickson College for 27 years before joining the administration of West Tennessee State Normal School. For many years, Loggins served as a member of the Tennessee State Board of Education, and was widely acquainted and well liked over the state of Tennessee. On the next day after his arrival, Loggins left in the company of President Mynders for Nashville and a meeting of the State Board of Education."

West Tennessee Normal School opened September 10, 1912 with Dr. Seymour A. Mynders as president. (U of M History) T. B. served as both the Dean and the head of the Mathematics Department. (Harold W. Stephens. "The Mathematics Department 1912-1973 A Brief History").

[The above picture was identified as a 1912 post card by http://www.historic-memphis.com/memphis-historic/normal-school/normal-school.html]

THE NORMAL SCHOOL PETS.

beds are used exclusively. Pupils furnish their own pillows, bed linen and bed cover.

The Southern Railroad has a depot, called Normal, located on the school grounds. If possible, when leaving home, buy tickets and have baggage checked to Normal. If you cannot do this, when you arrive at New Union Station, Memphis, buy ticket and re-check baggage to Normal. Then take street car and ask for transfer to Buntyn car. This will bring you direct to the school and save an expensive transfer.

INFORMATION.

Miss Jennie DeShazo has charge of Piano Teaching. Miss DeShazo has been trained in the best Conservatories of Europe and America, and as a teacher ranks among the best of this country.

Our Commercial Department is thoroughly equipped and has a course of study equal to the best.

For any further information, address Seymour A. Mynders, President, or T. B. Logging, Dean, Box 912, Memphis, Tenn.

Be sure to notify us when you are to arrive and you will be met at train in Memphis by a member of the faculty.

SUMMER TERM.

The six weeks Summer Term will begin the first week in June. A bulletin devoted to this alone will be issued in the early spring.

1912 Bulletin . The 2nd Bulletin - December 1912 .
Volume 1 . Number 4, page 15
[http://www.historic-memphis.com/memphis-historic/normal-school/bulletins/bulletins.html]

The 1913 Memphis Directory entry read: *"Loggins, Thos B. dean State Normal for West Tenn bds R. S. Thomas."* The abbreviation "bds" stood for "boards with." By the 1914 Memphis Directory listing, T. B. had moved to 182 S. Idlewild. The modern Zillow listing states that the house is a single family dwelling with four bedrooms and 2 baths with 2,568 square feet. The house was built in 1907.

Google Earth has a picture of the actual house. The current mileage to the University of Memphis is given as between four and five miles. The picture of the house was taken from the Google listing: https://www.google.com/maps/@35.1343871,-90.0018617,3a,75y,63.94h,101.5t/data=!3m6!1e1!3m4!1sutlH1MC9FHbRH132OhSSBw!2e0!7i13312!8i6656!6m1!1e1

Tragedy struck the West Tennessee Normal school on 17 September 1913 when Seymour A. Mynders died after serving as President of West Tennessee Normal for only one year. T. B., according to an article in The Golden Cross Journal, Volume XXXV, Number 7, Boston, Mass., December, 1913, p. 2 served as the "acting head" of WTNS:

> *"Friends and fellow-workers in the cause of education paid loving tribute to the memory of the late Capt. S. A. Mynders at the meeting of the City Club yesterday. .. Among those who spoke were...**Prof. T. B. Loggins, dean and acting head of the normal school"***

T. B. served only a short time before John Willard Brister became the president of West Tennessee Normal School. The 1914 Bulletin, Vol. III, No. 2, page 8 listed T. B. Loggins immediately below President Brister's entry in the Faculty section:

Thomas Billingsley Loggins, A. M. ....Dean, Mathematics--A. B. Glasgow Normal School; A. M., National Normal University; Teacher Mathematics, Edgewood Normal School, 1886-1889; President Dickson College, 1889-1911.

Pages 38 through 39 contained the Course outline and Course description for Department of Mathematics. The two teachers were

Professor Loggins and Miss Williams. T. B. taught Mathematics 20, 21, 22-Algebra; Mathematics 30, 31, 32-Plane Geometry-*"Special effort will be made to make geometry more interesting and more intelligible to the average student."*; Mathematics 40-Teacher's Arithmetic; Mathematics 50-Solid Geometry; Mathematics 51-Plane Trigonometry; Mathematics 52-College Algebra; and Mathematics 60, 61-Analytics.

Beth and Finis moved in with Addie and T.B before the 1914 Memphis Directory for Finis T. Rogers was listed as a Pharmacist for the Fortune-Ward Drug Co., with his residence at 182 S. Idlewild.

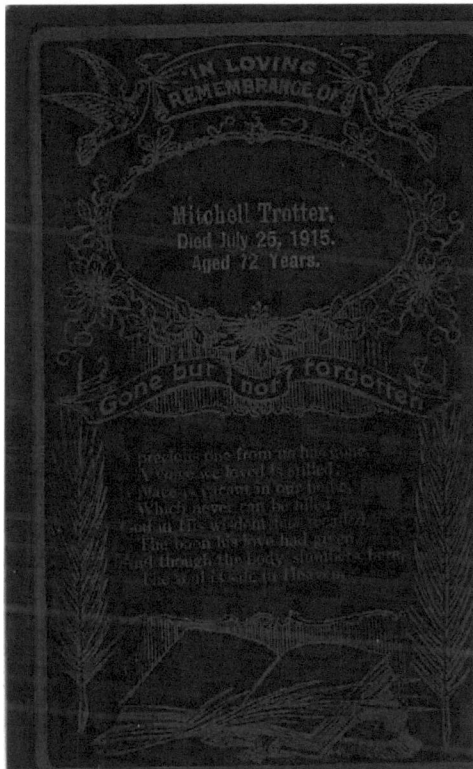

On 24 July, 1915, T. B. Loggins' maternal uncle, John Mitchell Trotter, Jr. died at the age of 71 years 6 months, and 16 days in Dickson, Tennessee with "organic heart disease." He was buried in Union Cemetery in Dickson, Tennessee in Heidelberg C, Lot 247. There is no owner listed for the plot on page 135 of the Union Cemetery Book but when the lot was purchased, T. B. was to be buried in Grave 1 and Addie in Grave 2. These plots remain unoccupied since Addie and T. B. are buried in Arizona. John Mitchell Trotter (8 December 1843-24 July 1915) is in Grave 7 and Lou Moore Trotter (19 June 1846-30 May 1931) is in Grave 8. In Grave 5 is T.B.'s brother, Walter Trotter Loggins(16 September 1872(WWI draft registration)-17 June 1936). W. T.'s wife is buried in Somerville. In Grave 6 is Lellie Trotter Miller (20 October 1869-1 May 1953. Lellie was the daughter of J. M. and Lou Trotter. Lellie's husband is buried in Memphis. Occupying graves 3 and 4 are bodies simply identified as Loggins. Who they are remains a mystery. (The Funeral card was part of R. B. and Zula Loggins collection now with

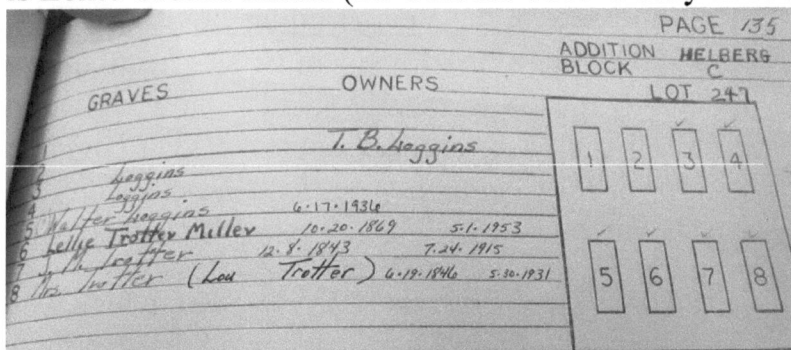

their descendants. Page 135 is from the Union Cemetery Book, Dickson, Tennessee.)
[According to a family story, In addition to losing their first child, Henry and Tera Eola Loggins gave birth to a set of twins who died at birth. The 1900 Census supports the loss of 3 children. I may never know if these Loggins' graves were that set of twins.]

The 1916 West Tennessee Normal School Bulletin Under Faculty on p. 7, "Thomas Billingsley Loggins, A.M.----Dean, Mathematics" listed the following information: *"A. B. Glasgow Normal School; A.M. National Normal University; Teacher Mathematics, Edgewood Normal School 1886-1889; President Dickson College, 1889-1911; present position since 1912."* Pages 56 through 58 listed the Department of Mathematics courses. This Bulletin used for the teachers the title Dean Loggins and Mr. Jones. Dean Loggins taught: Mathematics 20, 21, 22-Algebra; Mathematics 51-Plane Trigonometry; Mathematics 52-College Algebra; and Mathematics 60, 61-Analytics. On pages 8-18 Dean T. B. Loggins edits a section titled "Alumni Notes."

The 1916 Memphis Directory listed T. B. Loggins at 182 S. Idlewild and it also listed *"Rogers, Finis T. sec Fortune-Ward Drug Co"* with his residence as 182 S. Idlewild.

In 1916, Beth Loggins Rogers joined the Old Hickory Chapter, #747, of the United Daughters of the Confederacy in Dickson County, Tennessee. Her patriot was her paternal grandfather, Reuben Burch "R. B."Loggins. The form that Beth filled out to join the organization is the Tennessee State Archives. When Reuben Burch Loggins died is still unknown. He died after 1893 when he purchased items at the estate sale in Humphreys County, Tennessee of Samuel Larkins who was the father-in-law of his son, Henry Mitchell Loggins. His third wife, Mary Ann McGill Jarrell Loggins, whom he had married March 17, 1889 in Hustburg, was listed as a widow in the 1900 District 3 Humphreys County Census.

In the <u>Biennial Report of the State Superintendent of Public Education of Tennessee for the Years Ending June 30, 1915-1916</u> on page 170, President Brister listed the county meetings that the faculty had attended in the "Faculty Activities" section: *"Dean Loggins, four in Hardeman, one in Henderson, one in Shelby, two in Benton, and one in Decatur."*

Pages 10 and 11 of the 1916 <u>DeSoto</u>, which was the annual of the West Tennessee State Normal School, were the faculty pages. On page 10 in the composite picture, T. B. was pictured just right of the large picture of the President. T. B. was listed as "Thomas Billingsley Loggins, A. M., Dean....Mathematics." The 1917 DeSoto used individual faculty pictures in alphabetical order. "Thomas Billingsley Loggins, A. M., Dean, Mathematics" was on page 14. There was a cute little reference to T. B. on page 131 in the "Want Ads" section of the yearbook. "Wanted by Mr. Loggins--An automatic contrivance to remind Hugh Washburn to go to class."

[http://archive.org/stream/desoto191700unse#page/14/mode/2up]

The Bulletin for West Tennessee State Normal, Vol. VI, No. 1 that was published March 1917, listed the faculty on page 6. Thomas Billingsley Loggins was listed directly under President Brister's entry. T. B. continued to serve as Dean and teach Mathematics. For the summer session that was to be held June 11 through July 20, 1917, Dean Loggins was listed as teaching Mathematics 20-22 High School Algebra and Mathematics 51 or 52.

THE N.E.A. BULLETIN, SEPTEMBER 1917. p. 29 under the New Members/Tennessee section listed: T. B. Loggins, Dean State Normal School, Memphis, Tenn.

Addie was now a member of the National Society of the Daughters of the American Revolution, Commodore Perry Chapter, 3022 TN, in Memphis, Tennessee. She joined through the service of Robert Lindsay who gave Patriotic Service and Civil Service during the American Revolution.
"Mrs. Addie C. Loggins (T. B.)"was listed on the "Credential List" as an alternate for the Twenty-six Continental Congress of the National Society of the Daughters of the American Revolution that met in Washington, D. C. April 16, 1917. At some point during her membership in the TSDAR, Addie wrote a essay titled "Four Naval Heroes." That essay is in Box 32 #10 of Daughters of the American Revolution, Tennessee Society Records and Collected Materials 1894-2013 that is housed in the Tennessee State Archives. Beth Loggins Rogers and her cousin, Cammie Peeples Aldridge, joined the NSDAR later through the same Patriot.

Addie continued to be active in the Methodist Episcopal South Church. The following report was included in a Memphis Newspaper in 1918:
CHURCH AUXILARY
The Woman's Missionary study class of the First Methodist church will resume the regular twice-a-month study beginning Monday afternoon at

2 o'clock...Following the lesson the regular meeting of the entire membership will take place and a carefully arranged program will be rendered.

Those participating will be: Mrs. J. D. Wilson, devotional; Mrs. Grace Driver, vocal solo; Mrs. T. B. Loggins will give an address." The News Scimitar., November 09, 1918, 4th Edition, p.5.

note: Committee on Oriental Work continued from p. 12

NINTH ANNUAL MEETING.   13

Mrs. P. L. Cobb,	Mrs. Q. J. Rowley,
Miss Maud Henderson,	Mrs. T. B. Loggins, ⇦
Mrs. W. B. Higginbothem,	Mrs. W. T. Boswell,
Mrs. D. N. Bourne,	Dr. Hattie Love,
Mrs. C. F. Attersall,	Mrs. John N. Steele.

Ninth Annual Report of the Womans Missionary Council of The Methodist Episcopal Church, South, for 1918-1919

[Source: http://www.mocavo.com/Ninth-Annual-Report-of-the-Womans-Missionary-Council-of-the-Methodist-Episcopal-Church-South-for-1918-1919-Volume-1/926127/13]

The start of the school year on Monday, October 1, 1918 included another change in the President of West Tennessee State Normal School, but Thomas Billingsley Loggins remained the Dean. (If you are counting, this is the third President under whom T. B. served.) The new President, Andrew A. Kincannon, sent a most informative report to be included in Biennial Report of the State Superintendent of Public Education of Tennessee for the Years Ending June 30, 1917-1919. On page 97 he report about his inauguration as president and of the large number of young men who were admitted through the Students Army Training Corps. He listed the faculty beginning on page 97 with "T. B. Loggins, Dean, Professor of Mathematics" directly under his own listing. President Kincannon's description of the influenza epidemic was very interesting. The military authorities quarantined West Tennessee Normal at one point in the epidemic. Kincannon reported that although about 150 students suffered from Spanish Influenza, only one student died. At the end of the report, "A. A. Kincannon, President" commends the faculty for their "splendid efforts." during his most eventful first year.

T.B. Loggins stands among his students at West Tennessee Normal School in Memphis, Tennessee.
[Source: http://historic-memphis.com/memphis-historic/normal-school/normal-school.html]

The Bulletin for the 1918 year had stated that the school year would begin on September 23, 1918. The faculty was listed on page 5 with Thomas Billingsley Loggins' entry listed beneath President Kincannon's. The entry was the same as earlier bulletins. On page 10 was a listing of the faculty committees for the year. "Loggins" was listed as the first member of the following committees: Schedules, School Records, Teaching Positions, Credits and Advanced Standing. The Department of Mathematics section that began on page 59 listed Dean Loggins and Mr. Jones as the teachers. Dean Loggins taught Mathematics 20, 21, 22; Mathematics 51-Plane Trigonometry; Mathematics 52-College Algebra; Mathematics 60, 61-Analytics.

DICKSON NORMAL SCHOOL SALE

Recorded in Book 49, pages 56-57 was the sale of the Dickson Normal School Property.

" This Indenture made and entered into this the 19th day of February 1919 of the County of Shelby and State of Tennessee of the first part and G. W. Dodson of the second part; witnesseth[sic] that the said T. B. Loggins and wife Addie C. Loggins in consideration of the sum of Ten Thousand Dollars, of which Five Thousand Dollars is cash in hand paid...and for the balance said G. W. Dodson has made and delivered his Five several promissory notes of even date hence with for $1000.00 each payable 3, 6, 9, 12, and 15 mos after date ...the following described tract ...of land in Dickson County, State of Tennessee, to wit: in the Town of Dickson in the Fifth Civil District there of Beginning on a stake in what was J. Rickerts S.B. line, now Rickert Avenue and running South 32 degrees west 48 poles to a stone at a bearing S 41 degrees west 21 links from a large Spanish Oak pointer, and South 64 1/2degrees East 39 1/2 links from a large post oak pointer, and north 23 degree west 27 1/2 links from a Spanish Oak pointer, runs South 58 degrees East 28 poles and two links to a stone at a bearing of South three degrees East 18 links from a small black Jack, and South 56 degrees West 13 links from a small black oak bush pointer, then North 32 degrees East 66 3/5 poles to J Rickerts S. B. line, now Rickert Avenue. Thence west with said Rickerts line, Now Rickert Avenue, 34 poles to the beginning, containing TEN acres more or less (The same being the property deeded to W. T. Wade and T. B. Loggins by Mrs. Mary W. Cox, Deed Book "W" Pages 246 and 247.)The same property being since known as Dickson Normal College or Dickson College property together with all buildings apprentenances [sic], etc.,

According to H. Alan Ragan, Dickson County Historian, in his "Skits and Bits," that were tidbits gleaned from the Dickson County newspapers, the Dickson City Council had voted to buy the Dickson Normal School in February 1910 [February 7, 1910 issue], but it wasn't until April 1919 that the Dickson County Court voted to spend $8,250.00 to buy half of the property. Page 138 of From Mile Post 42... included the following paragraph:

"*A special meeting was called on April 9, 1919, for the purpose of considering a resolution relative to the purchase by the town of one-half of the T. B. Loggins School property from G. W. Dodson for the price of $8,250.00 said buildings to be used for a county high school, and on May 7, 1919, the ordinance presented at the April meeting was passed on first reading.*"

The City of Dickson paid the other half. The property was used for Central High School in Dickson. [April 7, 1919 issue and May 21, 1919 issue.] The January 16, 1931 issue carried the story of the fire that destroyed the old frame white building that had been used for the Girls' Dormitory. Many of the college records were destroyed in that fire. The May 20, 1964 issue stated that the brick building that Wade and Loggins had built circa 1892 was torn down in May. [The aerial view, on previous page, was in a prior to 1964 Dickson High School Yearbook. The building that was Dickson Normal College's Main Building is on the left forefront. The campus building faces College Street. The road beside the school on the left is now called Academy. The road at the back that Academy bends into in Rickert Avenue. The picture was posted to Discovering Dickson County Facebook page on February 12, 2016 by Chad Bradford.]

The July 1919 <u>Bulletin of West Tennessee Normal School, Vol. VIII, No. 3, Catalogue 1918-19 Announcement 1919-20</u> stated on the first page that the Eighth Year for the institution would begin Fall Term on September 22, 1919 and that Summer term would end July 17, 1920. [Note: W. T. Loggins, T. B.'s brother, was listed as the County Superintendent for Fayette County, Tennessee.] The Faculty list still had T. B. second after the president: *Thomas Billingsley Loggins, A.M., Dean, Mathematics; A.B. Glasgow Normal School; A.M., National Normal University; President Dickson College 1886-1912; Conductor Tennessee State Institutes 1896-1909; present position since 1912.* This year's catalogue listed the faculty by their length of time serving the college. Only four other faculty members had been associated with the school as long as T.B.: William E. Vaughan-English; Priestley Hartwell Manning-Physics and Geography; Helen Buquo-Home Economics; Clyde Hubert Wilson-Manual Training; and Mary Pettus Thomas-Modern Languages. Mrs. Seymour A. Mynders continued to serve as the Librarian. Pages 67-68 was devoted to the Mathematics Department. The teachers were Dean Loggins and Miss Proctor. Dean Loggins and Miss Proctor co-taught Mathematics 20,21,23-Algebra; Mathematics 40-Teacher's Arithmetic; and Mathematics 51-Plane Trigonometry. Dean Loggins taught Mathematics 52-College Algebra and Mathematics 60,61-Analytics

Attending the Summer Session of 1919 was Margaret Loggins of Lake County, Tennessee who was one of the seven daughters of T. B.'s brother, Will Loggins. Maggie, as she was known to the family, had a son named James Alexander "Alex" Leech. Dr. Leech served as the Madison County Executive (Tennessee) from 1982 until he retired in 2002. Two of Maggie's other sisters also attended West Tennessee Normal and became teachers. Minnie Loggins was listed in the 1922 West Tennessee State Normal School Bulletin. One of her most famous pupils in Lake county was Carl Perkins who in his autobiography said that "Miss Minnie" Loggins Lee, who was his early grade school teacher, arranged for him to sing at a school assembly. She even bought him a new white shirt for the occasion. Minnie went to Memphis State as an older adult to continue her education. Elizabeth "Baby" Loggins was listed in the 1928 and 1929 West Tennessee State Teachers' College Bulletin. Both women had long careers in education in Lake County, Tennessee. [WTNS became WTSTC became Memphis State is in 2016 University of Memphis]

There are a number of references to T. B. Loggins on the Library of Congress Chronicling America site during T. B.'s time at the West Tennessee Normal School. The references may be divided into three separate types of content: personal visits to T. B.'s brother, W. T. Loggins, who was the publisher of the Fayette Falcon in Somerville, Tennessee, business trips for West Tennessee Normal, and church activities of Addie:

Fayette Falcon, 5 March 1915, page 5 *"Prof. T. B. Loggins of the West Tennessee Normal school in Memphis was guest of his brother in Somerville last week."*

Fayette Falcon, 18 June 1915, page 5 *"Prof. and Mrs. T. B. Loggins of the State Normal School at Memphis were visitors in Somerville."*

Fayette Falcon: 9 June 1916, page 5 *"Prof and Mrs. T. B. Loggins of the West Tennessee Normal School were guests of local relatives this week."*

Fayette Falcon: 28 July 1916, page 5 "Prof. T. B. Loggins, dean of the faculty of the State Normal School in Memphis, was guest of local relatives here last Tuesday.

Fayette Falcon, 16 August 1918, page 5 *"Prof. T. B. Loggins of the West Tennessee Normal School at Memphis spent last Sunday in Somerville with relatives."*

[At this time there are no newspaper articles that record visits T. B. may have made to his brothers Will and Henry, but because Beth made trips back from Arizona to see her first cousins, we may assume that there were visits. A 1929 article in the Rutherford Register of Gibson County, Tennessee reported that W. T. was at the bedside of his terminally ill brother Henry so we know that the brothers remained close.]

Dresden enterprise and Sharon Tribune, September 11, 1914, page 6 *"Teacher's Big Rally Here---"after this, Prof. T. B. Loggins of Memphis, entertained us for a while in an interesting talk of general topics pertaining to better school work."*

Dresden Enterprise and Sharon Tribune, December 18, 1914, page 1: *"The Weakley County Teacher's association will meet in Dresden Saturday, Dec. 19. Below I give the program for the day: Dinner 1:30--Address by T. B. Loggins...Prof. T. B. Loggins of the West Tennessee Normal will be with us at each of the meetings for the remainder of the year and discuss the subject of arithmetic and its history."*

The Camden Chronicle, December 3, 1915, page 3: *"T. B. Loggins of the West Tennessee Normal, Memphis, was here Saturday."*

The Camden Chronicle, May 5, 1916, page 1: *"Teachers' Institute-The Benton County Teachers' Institute will begin Monday, May 22...The county teachers' meeting will be held on Saturday, May 29. The forenoon will be devoted to an address by Dean T. B. Loggins of the West Tennessee State Normal."*

The Camden Chronicle, May 19, 1916, page 3: *"The monthly teachers' meeting will be held Saturday, May 20. On this date Dean T. B. Loggins of the West Tennessee State Normal will address the teachers at 1 o'clock."*

Carroll County Democrat, September 14, 1917, page 4: *"Clarksburg High School-Prof. T. B. Loggins, of the Memphis normal, made a very interesting and profitable speech, and encouraged the good school projects with all the power to be had. Every person present pronounce it a wonderful speech."*

Fayette Falcon September 13, 1918, page 5: *"Prof. T. B. Loggins, Dean of the West Tennessee Normal School, will be at The Falcon office Saturday, Sept 1r, from early morning until 2 p. m. for the purpose of giving such information as is desired by young men 18 to 21 who want to enter the military department of that school under the U. S. Government plan. Such young men will have their expenses paid and will be paid regular army pay, $30 per month. Such as desire information can discuss the matter with him during Saturday at The Falcon office."*

Fayette Falcon , September 20, 1918, page 5: *"Nearly a score of Fayette County boys of draft age registered last Saturday with Prof. T. B. Loggins, Dean of the West Tennessee Normal School, who was in Somerville for that purpose. A number of others from this and other vicinities in the county had already registered and will enter the school when it begins its new term the first of October."*

The Covington Leader, December 5, 1918, page 6: *Mrs. T. P. Davidson, of Abilene, Tex; Mr. H. P. Cotten, of Rives; Mr. J. A. Cotten, Jr. of Memphis; Mr. A. S. Cottten, Prof. T. B. Loggins, Messrs A. A. Miller and P. H. Manning, of Memphis, were here Sunday to attend the funeral of Prof. J. A. Cotten."*

Fayette Falcon April 25, 1919, page 1: *"Thirty teachers in public schools of the county met last Saturday at the High School building here for their monthly institute. Prof. T. B. Loggins, Dean of the Faculty of the West Tennessee Normal , talked on Arithmetic as it relates to actual business and the defects of our system of teaching it."*

 (Addie) Dresden Enterprise and Sharon Tribune, October 10, 1919, page 7: *"Woman's Mission Society of the M. E. Church meeting at Sharon on October 16-17: October 17, 2 p. m. Life Service-- Mrs. T. B. Loggins"*

(Addie) Lawrence Democrat, December 18, 1912, page 5: *Mrs. T. B. Loggins of Dixon, a prominent missionary worker of the M. E. church will be the guest of Dr. and Mrs. D. T. Gould for several days."*

(Addie) The News Scimitar (Memphis, Tennessee), November 9, 1918: *Church Auxiliary...of the First Methodist church"..."Mrs. T. B. Loggins will give and address."*

T. B. left West Tennessee State Normal School at the end of the 1919-1920 school year. His son-in-law, Finis T. Rogers, had contracted Tuberculosis. Finis and Beth moved to Phoenix, Arizona in hopes that Finis' health would improve. T. B. and Addie moved to Phoenix to be with Beth and Finis. The DeSoto yearbook staff dedicated the 1920 annual to T. B. (The illustration is a composite of the pages from the yearbook.)

De Soto Vol III

Edited by
The Senior Class
of
West Tennessee
State Normal School
1920

Thomas Billingsley Loggins
A. B.
A. M.

Dedication

This volume of the DeSoto is dedicated in respect for his loyal and warm-hearted work for the institution and in appreciation for his constant interest in our welfare, to

Thomas Billingsley Loggins

On June 14, 1920, T. B. sold one lot in the George J. Campbell Subdivision to Pauline and Peter Henry Kemp. The type on the deed that is available on Tom Leatherwood, Register of Shelby County Deeds web page is difficult to read but the streets bordering the property were Allen St., Idlewild, and the old line of Union Avenue. The lot number is not legible. The deed was recorded in Book 0759, p. 187. [One is able to access the deed on this site by searching Loggins, T. B.] A few days later, on June 23, 1920, T. B. and Addie sold Lot 9 in the George J. Campbell Subdivision to Elsie Gardner Watkins. The streets mentioned were Idlewild and Union Avenue. This deed was recorded in Book 0763, p. 42.

Page 332 of the 1921 Phoenix City directory listed "Loggins, Thos B (Addie C) h 2244 N 7th." Page 425 of that same directory listed "Rogers, Finis T (Beth L) h 2244 N 7th."

Sadly, Finis' health did not improve. His obituary was reported in the Arizona Republic published in Phoenix, Arizona on September 2, 1921, page 6.

OBITUARIES: Finis T. Rogers, of 2244 North Seventh street, died on Wednesday morning at Globe where he went about four weeks ago. He was 30 years of age and is survived by his wife. Mr. and Mrs. "Rogers, accompanied by Mrs. Rogers' parents, Mr. and Mrs. T. B. Loggins, came to Phoenix about a year ago from Memphis, Tennessee, for Mr. Rogers' health. Funeral services will be held at the A. H. McLellan Chapel at 3 o'clock this afternoon conducted by the Rev. C. M. Aker, pastor of Central Methodist Church. The Masons will officiate at Greenwood cemetery.

Source: https://www.newspapers.com/newspage/119330228/

Beth Loggins Rogers was named the executor of Finis' estate. All the paper work may be found in the Arizona Wills and Probate Records, 1803-1995 for Finis T. Rogers, Maricopa County, Case files P4303-P4351." In the Inventory section was the following: *"That portion of Lot one (1), Baltimore Heights, a subdivision on the Southeast quarter of the Northeast quarter of Section 32, Township 2, North, Range 3 East of the Gila and Salt River Base and Meridian, in the County of Maricopa, State of Arizona, according to the map...Book 2, of Maps, at page 67."* The lot was appraised at Forty-Five Hundred dollars.

T. B. appeared to have withdrawn from education once he went to Phoenix. The searches of his name in Arizona yielded very few results. Although I'm sure that there was correspondence to his brothers and their families, I have found none.

An interesting use of T. B.'s name was in Business Arithmetic that was published in 1922 by Preston Edmond Curry, Victor M. Rubert.
Exercise examples: "16. Sold merchandise to T. B. Loggins, on account, $98.82 25. Sold merchandise to T. B. Loggins, on account, $160.00."
On April 6, 1922, T. B.'s oldest brother, William Nicholas "Will" Loggins died with Bright's Disease in Tiptonville, Tennessee. Will's birth date was listed as August 5, 1859 in Mississippi. Will's oldest daughter, Justa Loggins was the informant. She listed Will's parents as Reuben Loggins of Mississippi and Mary E. Trotter of Mississippi. His occupation was farmer.

In 1924, Addie was quite active in her church work. Page 2 of the July 24, 1924 issue and Page 14 of the December 23, 1924 issue of the Arizona Republic carried stories about her work in the Methodist Church's women's work. T. B. gave brief talk to the ladies of the Central Methodist

Church according to page 30 of the March 16, 1924 issue of the <u>Arizona Republic.</u> In the April 25, 1925 issue of the <u>Arizona Republic,</u> Mrs. T. B. Loggins presented a program titled "Testaments Up the Sleeves and Testaments in the Heart" for the women's meeting of the church.

Photo taken in 2013 by ARMLS

"Listing Agent, Christopher A. Paris: WELCOME TO 30 E VERNON AV IN DOWNTOWN PHOENIX'S ASHLAND PLACE HISTORIC DISTRICT. STORYBOOK 1928 TUDOR W/ NEWER SHAKE ROOF (2003) ON A QUIET TREE-LINED STREET 1 BLOCK FROM THE HEARD MUSEUM & LIGHT RAIL STATION ON CENTRAL AV. MANY ORIGINAL FEATURES INCLUDING HARDWOOD FLOORS, BARREL CEILINGS, GAS & WOOD-BURNING FIREPLACE, WOOD-FRAMED WINDOWS, BUILT-IN BOOKCASES & MUCH MORE!" [Source: http://www.zillow.com/homedetails/30-E-Vernon-Ave-Phoenix-AZ-85004/7536474_zpid/]

In the 1925 Phoenix Directory, T.B., Addie and Beth were still living at 2244 N.7th. The listing was still using Finis T. Rogers with Elizabeth in parentheses. By the 1928 directory, the three of them had moved to 810 N. 5th. Beth was listed as Mrs. Beth Rogers, teacher.

The 1929 Phoenix Directory listed another move for the threesome. They were now living at 30 E. Vernon Avenue. This house still existed in 2013.

The 31 October 1929 Arizona Republic carried the following story on page 20 about a visit from T.B.'s brother, R. B. Loggins:

" Guests were Mr and Mrs. T. B. Loggins and Mr. and Mrs. F. T. Rogers, Phoenix, Mr. and Mrs. R. B. Loggins, R. B. Loggins, Jr., and Miss Eugenia Pierce, West Columbia, Texas."

The 1929 and 1930 Phoenix Directories listed T. B. and Addie, in addition, the directory identified T. B. as a teacher. I have not been able to find any proof that he was actually teaching in Phoenix.

On July 18, 1929, T. B. lost his brother, Henry Mitchell Loggins who was about two years older than he. Henry, a farmer and Elder in the Yorkville Cumberland Presbyterian Church died in his home just one mile, going toward Newbern, outside Yorkville, Tennessee. He died from an infection in the left cerebral cortex. The informant was the husband of his daughter, Sammie Loggins Farrar. L. E. Farrar listed Henry's parents as Reuben B. Loggins of Alabama and Mary Trotter of Tennessee. Henry's birth was listed as November 18, 1860 in Lodi, Mississippi. Henry was buried in the Yorkville Cemetery. [Note: Henry's and Tillman's death certificates were the only ones that had the correct birth places for their parents.]

August 20, 1931, T. B. Loggins signed a letter of Administration for the estate of Martha Louisa Moore Loggins who had named T. B. as the executor of her estate.

Phoenix, Arizona, August 20th, 1931.

TO THE HONORABLE COUNTY COURT
OF DICKSON COUNTY, TENNESSEE:

I, T. B. Loggins, the undersigned, solemnly swear that I will faithfully perform the "Will" of LOU TROTTER, deceased, according to law, to the best of my skill and ability, so help me God.

T. B. Loggins,

Subscribed and sworn to before me J.M.Kellogg, a Notary Public in and for Maricopa County, at Phoenix, Arizona, by T. B. Loggins on August 20th, 1931.

Notary Public.

My commission expires
January 14th, 1934.

> Probate Records for M. Loe Trotter in Administrative Bonds and Letters, 1912-1949, page 3

Addie Campbell Loggins died November 4, 1935. According to her Maricopa, Arizona Death Certificate, she died from kidney failure due to Chronic Nephritis. The following were published in the Arizona Republic:

November 5, 1935, page 6: "*Mrs. Addie Loggins Dies At Home Here. Mrs. Addie C. Logins, resident of Phoenix for the past 15 years, died last night at her home, 30 East Vernon street. Mrs. Loggins who was 71 years old. had a wide circle of friends in the city. She is survived by her husband, T. B. Loggins and daughter, Mrs. Beth L. Rogers of Phoenix: . Funeral arrangements will be announced later by the A. H. McLellan Mortuary.*

November 6, 1935, page 12:

Addie C Loggins Passed away November 4 at her home, 30 East Vernon street. Funeral services will be conducted this afternoon at 3:30 from the A. H. McLellan chapel with the Rev. William H. Coleman officiating.

On June 17, 1936, T. B.'s baby brother died in Shelby County, Tennessee. Walter Trotter Loggins was in the Home For the Incurables in Memphis, Tennessee. He died from a cerebral hemorrhage, but the doctor said that W. T. had been suffering from Paralysis, which at the time was the diagnosis often given for strokes. His death certificate was sketchy because it was filled out by the hospital. As already mentioned, W.T. was buried in the Union Cemetery in Dickson, Tennessee.

On March 10, 1939, T.B.'s younger brother, "Judge Reuben Burch Loggins" died in West Columbia, Brazoria County, Texas. R.B.'s son, G. E. Loggins, signed as informant on the death certificate. R. B.'s birth date was given as September 25, 1865 in Lodi, Mississippi. His parents were listed as R. B. Loggins of Mississippi and Mary Trotter of Mississippi. His profession was listed as attorney. He died of a cerebral hemorrhage. He was buried in the cemetery in West Columbia, Texas. [R.B. Loggins has the wrong Roman numeral on his stone, but the other information is correct.]

After having lived 77 years, 11 months, and 26 days, Thomas Billingsley Loggins died September 27, 1940 in the Clark's Rest Home in Phoenix, Arizona of a Cerebral Hemorrhage. He had been a patient there for a month according to his death certificate. His daughter, Mrs. Beth L. Rogers, was the informant. He had resided in Arizona for nineteen years. His usual occupation was listed as Dean of West Tennessee Teachers' College. His parents were listed as Rubin L. Loggins of Mississippi and Mary Trotter of Mississippi. He was buried in the Greenwood Cemetery in Phoenix.

The death notice for T. B. that was published in the September 28, 1940 Issue of the Arizona Republic, page 20 was hardly a fitting memorial for a man who had spent his life educating thousands of young people, many of whom became educators, nor did the death notice say that the only surviving brother resided in Angleton, Texas.

LOGGINS, Thomas B., father of Mrs. Beth L. Rogers and brother of J. T. Loggins, passed away Thursday at a local hospital. Services at 2:30 p. m. today from Memory Chapel of A. L. Moore and Sons, with the Rev. James B. Curry officiating. Interment at Greenwood.

The last of the six Loggins Boys, James Tillman Loggins, died January 31, 1942 in Angleton, Texas of Hypertensive Heart Disease. His wife, Ethel McCauley Loggins, signed as informant. [Since Ethel was originally from Hustburg and not only knew Tillman's parents, but was a member of Tillman's maternal family, she was the most credible of all the death certificate informants.] She listed his trade as lawyer and his industry as law and insurance. He was born December 25, 1866 in Lodi, Mississippi. His parents were Reuben B. Loggins of Alabama and Mary Elizabeth Trotter of Tennessee. He was buried in the Angleton, Cemetery.

Circa 1937, Beth Loggins Rogers, came "home" to Tennessee for a visit. There was a grand family reunion held in Lake County. My mother, Bettye Jean Loggins McCaffrey Ellis, remembers the fun they had during Beth's visit. Seven of William Nicholas Loggins' children were in attendance, but only three of Henry's children made the gathering: Reuben Wilson Loggins who was the tallest man in the back, Pearl Loggins Hall who was the woman in the dark dotted dress, and Tucker who was the woman on the far right. My mother was the little girl in the dress with the bow. Beth, as the guest of honor, stood in the middle in front of Granddaddy Reuben and directly behind the seated man in the hat.

Beth Loggins Through the Years

Top left: R. Poole Portraits, Nashville, Cor. Cherry and Union-hand written caption read "Uncle Reuben and Aunt Zula from Beth" (R.B. and Zula's collection); Top Middle: Thuss, Nashville, Tenn. (R.B. and Zula's collection) Top Right: Thuss, 230 N. Cherry, Nashville, Tenn., caption given by my grandmother, Grace Edwards Loggins to Gwen in 1979 "Beth Loggins, Uncle T. B.'s daughter, Grandpa Loggins' niece"; Bottom left: Thuss &Koellien, Corner of College and Union Streets, Nashville, Tenn. (Henry and Tera's collection); Bottom Middle: Nashville, Tenn. but studio not clear (R.B. and Zula's collection); Bottom Right: from collection of her first cousin, Reuben Wilson Loggins, that was made the day of the circa 1937 Family Reunion in Lake County, Tennessee.

Beth Campbell Loggins Rogers never remarried. She served as the librarian for Phoenix Union High School until her retirement. Her obituary in the May 14, 1986 <u>Arizona Republic,</u> page 21:

> *Beth L. Rogers, 95, a retired librarian for Phoenix Union High School, died May 11, 1986, at Beatitudes Campus Care Center. Mrs. Rogers, of Phoenix, was born in Lodi, Miss., and moved to Arizona in 1920 from Tennessee. She attended Ward Belmont College and George Peabody College Library Department. Survivors include cousins and friend, Leta Weaver. Friends may call from 5 to 8 p.m. today at A.L. Moore & Sons 333 W. Adams. Services will at 2 p.m. Thursday at Central United Methodist Church, 1875 N. Central. Memorial contributions may, be made to the Central United Methodist Church, 1875 N. Central. Phoenix 85004.*

I end as I began with Beth Campbell Loggins Rogers standing together for a picture with her first cousin, Reuben Wilson Loggins, Sr.

This was quite a get together. The children, grandchildren and great grandson of Loggins Brothers, Will, Henry, and T. B., came together from Florida, Arizona, Missouri, and Tennessee in Maggie's Tiptonville, Tennessee yard in the late 1940's. On Ground: Johnny Loggins who is the grandson of Will and son of Luten. On the Bench left to right: Dickie Moore who is the great grandson of Henry and the grandson of Hugh, Will's daughter Lois, Will's daughter Verna, Will's son Luten. Standing: Will's daughter Minnie, Hugh's wife Alma, Will's daughter Maggie, Henry's son Reuben, T.B.'s daughter Beth Loggins Rogers, Henry's daughter Sam, and Reuben's wife Grace.

The caption on the back of this photograph read: Mag, Lute, Sam, Lois, Verna, Beth, Reuben & Minnie.

May 13, 2016-I give my thanks to the following people for helping to make this little book a reality: Beth Loggins Roberts who is the granddaughter of R. B. and Zula Loggins; Jeff Wills of the Dickson County Library Genealogy Room; Alan Ragan of the Dickson County Historical Society; Pam Edwards of the Dickson County, Tennessee Archives; Jack Wood and Evelyn Keel of the Tennessee Room of the Jackson Madison County Library; the countless people who make information available on the internet; Matt and Susan Knight Gore, and my husband who acts as my chauffer and sounding board.
Gwendolyn McCaffrey McReynolds

The Other Brothers, Their Spouses, and Children

Henry Mitchell Loggins' Family 1920 Yorkville, TN--Standing: The Triplets (1900): Pearl, Pierce, Pauline; Addie Bowen (1897); Reuben Wilson (1892) Sammie (1888); Chairs: Mary (1885); Hugh (1883) Tera Eola Larkins Loggins; Henry; Ground: Tucker (1902)
(Photo from the collection of Gwen McCaffrey McReynolds)

1930's Brazoria Co., Texas: **James Tillman "J. T." Loggins**, Ethel McCauley Loggins, Zula Winstead Loggins, **Reuben Burch "R. B."Loggins, Jr.**

(Photo from the collection of

R.B. and Zula's grandchildren, Burch and Beth Roberts)

126

Photograph of R. B. Loggins in his law office in Columbia, Brazoria County, Texas. He sent this picture to his brother, Henry Loggins. It is now in the collection of Henry's great granddaughter, Gwen. The picture below is of Reuben Burch and Zula Loggins' two sons, Reuben Burch Loggins, III with his daughter Elizabeth "Beth" Loggins and George Ethelred Loggins.

William Nicholas Loggins' and wife, Kate Luten Loggins' Children: Justa (1890); Verna (1892); Reuben Luten "Luten" (1894); Margaret "Maggie" (1895); Kate (1897); Minnie (1900); Lois (1901); Baby (1905) [Baby's legal name was Elizabeth but she even went by Miss Baby when she taught school in Tiptonville.]

Walter Trotter Loggins' and Jennie Cocke Loggins' son: James Elwyn Loggins (1894) This photograph of young James Elwyn was taken by J. H. Moyston of Memphis, Tennessee. The picture was sent to his Uncle R. B. and Aunt Zula in Columbia, Texas. James Elwyn attended both Vanderbilt Law school and George Washington University. He served during World War I. He also served as a lawyer for the Veteran's Administration. Eventually he served as the Chief Secretary for the Veteran's Bureau in Washington, D. C.

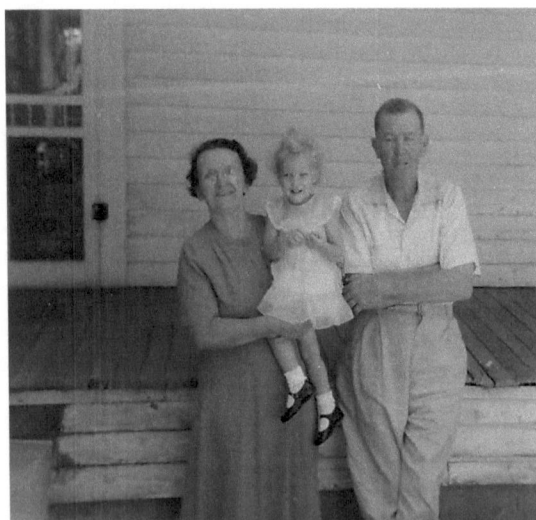

Gwendolyn McCaffrey McReynolds' lineage: Reuben Burch and Mary Elizabeth Trotter Loggins to Henry Mitchell and Tera Eola Larkins Loggins to Reuben Wilson and Grace Edwards Loggins to Bettye Jean Loggins McCaffrey and husband, James Robert McCaffrey, to Gwen. [Gwen with Granddaddy Reuben and Grandmother Grace about 1956]

128

Appendix

The following is the complete list by E. B. Wilson, the institute secretary, of those who participated in the Four Week Tennessee State Teachers Institute that was held at the Dickson Normal College in 1904. Conductor, T. B. Loggins noted in his report that there were a total number of 184 enrolled with students from thirteen Middle Tennessee Counties and seven from West Tennessee Counties.

ANNUAL REPORT OF THE STATE SUPERINTENDENT OF PUBLIC INSTRUCTION FOR TENNESSEE FOR THE SCHOLASTIC YEAR ENDING JUNE 30, 1904, Pp. 114-119

HONOR ROLL: Alice Wilson Blackwell (Dickson), Mary Bussell (Columbia), Eva Claggette (Little Lot); J. F. Duncan (Martin), Eva Mildred English (Dickson), R. E. Gorham (White Bluff), **Mrs. Alice E. Hickman (Union City)** *[Note: She is on the faculty of DNC in 1911.]* Fannie Montgomery (Martin), Gertrude Rogers (Cordova), W. M. Stewart (Burns), R. C. White (Stayton), Nina Belle Taylor (Eaton), Mrs. Della C. Nicholson (Eaton)*[This was an error for she is listed as Trenton in the Institute list.]*

INSTITUTE ROLL: W.M. Adcock (White Bluff, Dickson Co.), Ether Adkins (Yellow Creek, Houston, Co.) Nevada Baird (Lyle, Hickman Co.), C. J. Baker (Pomp, Hickman Co.), O. E. Baker (Dickson, Dickson Co.), Jessie Basford (Oakplain, Montgomery Co.), Mattie Basford (Oakplain, Montgomery Co.), W. M. Bateman (Sylvia, Dickson Co.), Jennie Beard (Lyle, Hickman Co.), Ida Beasley (Dickson, Dickson Co.), Gertrude Berry (Dickson, Dickson Co.), D. A. Bishop (Tennessee City, Dickson Co.), Alice Blackwell (Dickson, Dickson), J. E. Brock (Bellsburg, Dickson), Aura E. Burcham (Charter's Creek, Maury Co.), Agnes Buquo (Dickson, Dickson), Lee Bussell (Abiff, Hickman Co.), Mary Bussell (Columbia, Maury Co.), Willie Briggs (Dickson, Dickson), Jennie Carman (Beffrange, Dickson Co.), J. T. Campbell (Dickson, Dickson), Vera Carr (Burns, Dickson), Eva Claggette (Little Lott, Hickman Co.), Choe Clement (Dickson, Dickson), Dora Clement (Dickson, Dickson), Daisy Cobb (Big Rock, Stewart Co.), Ethel Collier (Stewart, Houston Co.), Nellie Collier (Stewart, Houston Co.)Bessie Comperry (Sango, Montgomery Co.), Allie Cooper (Bon Aqua, Hickman Co.), Eva Corlew (Charlotte, Dickson Co.), R. E. Corlew (Dickson, Dickson), Nora Cotter (Sylvia, Dickson Co.), Ann Coulter (Burns, Dickson Co.), Minnie Coulter (Burns, Dickson Co.), Ruby Crumplery (White Bluff, Dickson Co.), Hattie Cunniff (Dickson, Dickson), A. J. Dean (Vanleer, Dickson Co.), Joe E. Dickson (Vanleer, Dickson Co.),

John E. Dickson (Slayden, Dickson Co.), Alva Dixon (Cunningham, Montgomery Co.), J.F. Duncan (Martin, Weakley Co.), Bessie Dunn (Franklin, Williamson Co.), Easley, Ernest (Dickson, Dickson), Essie Easley (Dickson, Dickson), Fannie Edwards (blank), Mildred English (Dickson, Dickson), Ollie Ferrell (Dickson, Dickson), Alice Fowler (Dickson, Dickson), Amanda Few (Dickson, Dickson), J. A. Fielder (Dickson, Dickson), Susie Fields (Martin, Weakley Co.), Percy B. Freeman (Dickson, Dickson), Ida Gerlicher (Theodore, Perry Co.), Augusta Guerin (Dogwood, Montgomery Co.), Myrtle Gilbert (Bellsburg, Dickson Co.), M. H. Goldston (Peryear, Henry Co.), R. E. Gorham (White Bluff, Dickson Co.), Rebecca Gray (Moltke, Stewart Co.), Thos. J. Greer (Charlotte, Dickson Co.) Stella Gross (Stewart, Houston Co.), Maude Groves (Little Rock Mills, Hickman Co.), Ira Gunson (Cumberland City, Stewart Co.) Era Hammon (Spencer Mills, Dickson Co.), Leora Harder (Beardstown, Perry County), W. S. Harper, Dogwood, Montgomery Co.), Earley Harris (Petway, Cheatham Co.), Melvin Harris (Charlotte, Dickson Co.), Lena Herron (Dickson, Dickson), **Mrs. Alice E. Hickman (Union City, Obion Co.)** Alice Higdon (Dickson, Dickson), Susie Hogin (Burns, Dickson Co.), Mrs. Mary Hooper (Slayton, Dickson Co.), Virgil Hunt (Dickson, Dickson), Willie C. Hutton (Dickson, Dickson), J. L. Hutcherson (Aden, Williamson Co.), Winfield Jarrett (Bellsburg, Dickson Co.), Ethel Jobe (Beefrange, Dickson Co.), Cleveland Jones (Newbern, Dyer Co.), Maude Jones (McEwen, Humphreys Co.), R. B. Killebrew (Dresden, Weakley Co.), Geneva King (Bailey, Shelby Co.), Magenta King (Bailey, Shelby Co.), Nina Kinnie (Franklin, Williamson Co.), **Faustina Larkins (Charlotte, Dickson Co.), Milbria Larkins (Charlotte, Dickson Co.),** S. M. Larkins (Dickson, Dickson), **Addie C. Loggins (Dickson, Dickson)**, J. W. Long (Woods Valley, Dickson Co.), Mrs. Inez Long (Wood Valley, Dickson Co.), Doy Lowrey (Dickson, Dickson), Emma Martin (Dickson, Dickson) Etta Martin (Dickson, Dickson), Ada McAulay (Erin, Houston Co.), D. J. McCauley (Erin, Houston Co.), Fannie McMillan (Charlotte, Dickson Co.) Nora McMillan (Charlotte, Dickson Co.), Margarette Merryman (Waverly, Humphreys Co.), Henrie Miles (Martin, Weakley Co.), Obera Mintun (Kenton, Gibson Co.), Fannie Montgomery (Martin, Weakley Co.), Bettie Moore (Johnsonville, Humphreys Co.), Susie Moore (Johnsonville, Humphreys Co.), Millie Moore (Dickson, Dickson), Sarah F. Moore (Johnsonville, Humphreys Co.), W. E. Moore (Clifton, Wayne Co.), Bennie Philip Morrison (Nashville, Davidson Co.), W. J. Morrison (Centreville, Hickman Co.), Mamie E. Myatt (White Bluff, Dickson Co.), Hayes Mitchell (Vanleer, Dickson Co.), L. P. Nichols (Omega, Houston Co.), Mrs. Della Nicholson (Trenton, Gibson Co.), Frank Nicks (Charlotte,

Dickson Co.), Cecile Pack (Dull, Dickson Co.), Dollie Proch (Bakerville, Humphreys Co.), Minnie Pack (Dull, Dickson Co.) West Page (Deepspring, Cheatham Co.), Judson Palmer (Dickson, Dickson), Alice Patton (Bon Aqua, Hickman Co.), Loula Payne (Dickson, Dickson), Jennie Payne (Dickson, Dickson), D. G. Pentecost (Palmersville, Weakley Co.), **Ellis Perdue (Franklin, Kentucky)** [note: He is on the faculty in 1905.] W. R. Philps (Union City, Obion Co.), M. W. Plant (Plant, Humphreys Co.), Arthur Poore (Centreville, Hickman Co.), T. S. Register (Dickson, Dickson), Maggie Reynolds (Dickson, Dickson), Ida Reynolds (Dickson, Dickson), Pinor Reynolds (Vanleer, Dickson Co.), Ethel Ridings (Woolworth, Humphreys Co.), Evie Ridings (Woolworth, Humphreys Co.), Clara Richardson (Burns, Dickson Co.), Mabel Richmond (Germantown, Shelby Co.), Bessie Rickert (Dickson, Dickson), N. O. Robbin (Erin, Houston Co.), J. A. Roberson (Waynesboro, Wayne Co.), Gertrude Rogers (Cordova, Shelby Co.), Cooper Sanders (Troy, Obion Co.), Onie Sensing (Dull, Dickson Co.), S. L. Smith (Clarksville, Montgomery Co.) Belle Smithson (Witham, Sumner Co.), Willie Sparkman (Linden, Perry Co.), Mollie Spencer (Burns, Dickson Co.), Scott Stephenson (Centerville, Hickman Co.), W. N. Stewart (Burns, Dickson Co.), Minnie Story (Dull, Dickson Co.), Ernest Sugg (Dickson, Dickson), Nina Swift (McEwen, Humphreys Co.), W. R. Tarr (Aden, Williamson Co.), Chas Taylor (Charlotte, Dickson Co.), Marvin Taylor (Dickson, Dickson), Myrtle Taylor (Vanleer, Dickson Co.), Nina Belle Taylor (Eaton, Crockett Co.), Roscoe Thomas (Dickson, Dickson), B. C. Thomasson (Clarksville, Montgomery Co.), Nannie Thompson (Burns, Dickson Co.), Ethel Tidwell (Burns, Dickson Co.), Maurice Tidwell (Bon Aqua, Hickman Co.), C. J. Tidwell (Dickson, Dickson), Bertha Vanhook (Beefrange, Dickson Co.), R. F. Wall (Beefrange, Dickson Co.), T. J. Warren (Dickson, Dickson), Maggie Watson (Vanleer, Dickson Co.), T. W. Weems (Tidwell, Dickson Co.), Clara White (Burns, Dickson), Norvia White (Burns, Dickson Co.), Prudence White (Spencers Mill, Dickson Co.), R. C. White (Stayton, Dickson Co.), W. M. White (Dickson, Dickson), A. H. Wiggs (Beardstown, Perry Co.), Della Williams (Dickson, Dickson), Freddie Wolf (White Bluff, Dickson Co.), **Mosie Wyatt (Hustburg, Humphreys Co.)**, Minnie Wynns (Dickson, Dickson), Mrs. Alma Yates (Plant, Humphreys Co.), I. H. Young (Bold Springs, Humphreys Co.)

Reuben Burch Loggins, Jr.'s November, 1887 letter of reference from Danville, Tennessee. [Houston County, Tennessee.] The letter is in the possession of Beth Loggins Rogers. After contacting Melissa Barker Certified Archival Records Manager Houston County, TN., I learned that Danville school was in District 1 of Houston County. Research into the signature of W. F. Grafried was quite productive. He lived in Danville. He was born, according to his death record in Switzerland. The 1880 District 1, Houston County census said Baden and the 1900 District 1 Houston County census stated Germany. His full name was William Frederick Grafried. His daughter, Clara, became a school teacher. She taught school for forty years.

A. Cathey may have been Archibald

Danville Tenn Nov. 7 / 87.
To whom it may concern.

Whereas Prof. R. B. Loggins, who has been connected with the schools of our district for some time past, as principal, has in the exercise of his judgement, as to what is best to promote his own interests, severed his connection with said schools; and whereas we, the of directors, of said district desire to give some expression to our high appreciation of his worth as a teacher and

Cathey, a farmer of District 1, Houston County.

gentleman, therefore

Resolved, That we as a
board of directors cheer-
fully bear testimony to
the manly character of
Prof. Loggins to the high
esteem in which he is
held by the citizens of
this community to his
great efficiency as a
teacher, and to the em-
inent success which
attended his efforts
in building up and
sustaining our school.

Resolved further, That
we regard Prof. Loggins
as a true gentleman
and a teacher of excel-
lent qualifications and
attainments, and we so
recommend him to
all whom it may con-
cern. It is with the
profoundest regret that
we part with him and
lose his services in
behalf of our school
Our best wishes for
his success and happi-
ness, will follow him
into whatever field
of labor he may go.

Resolved further, That
we regard Prof. Loggins
as a true gentleman
and a teacher of excel
lent qualifications and
attainments. and we so
recommend him to
all whom it may con
cern— It is with the
prof'oundest regret that
we part with him and
lose his services in
behalf of our school
Our best wishes for
his success and happi
ness, will follow him
into whatever field
of labor he may go.
Resolved, That the sec
retary of this board
furnish a copy of
these resolutions to
Prof. Loggins.

          W. F. Graffried Sec.
          A. Cathey, Pres.

www.ingramcontent.com/pod-product-compliance
Lightning Source LLC
Chambersburg PA
CBHW060801270326
41926CB00002B/48